a place for ALPACAS

A Place for Alpacas

Text, photographs & graphics
copyright © Cilla Taylor 2012

ISBN 13: 978-1470084622

All rights reserved. No part of this publication may be reproduced, stored in a retrieval system or transmitted in any form or by any means (electronic, mechanical, or by photocopying, recording or otherwise), without the prior permission of the copyright owner.

Cilla Taylor

a place for
ALPACAS

CONTENTS

Introduction	**7**
Background and History	**9**
Background	9
History	11
First imports	12
Ruminants	12
Life span	13
Behaviour	**16**
Alpaca behaviour	16
Communications	25
Moving your alpacas	26
Halter training	26
The Farm Environment	**30**
Stocking ratio	30
Fences	30
Yards and pens	32
Shelter	33
Poisonous trees and plants	36
Annoying plants and fleece contamination	40
Health	**43**
Body scoring	43
Worming	44
Toenail trimming	47
Teeth	49
Vitamin D and rickets	49
Ryegrass staggers	51
Skin conditions	53
PEM	53
Grain overload	54
Facial Eczema	54
Rabbit holes and broken bones	56
TB and Johnes Disease	57
Poisoning	57
Infections and abnormal temperature	58
Support groups	59
Shearing	**60**
Shearing your alpacas	60
Understanding fleece test results	62
Breeding	**64**
Breeding age	64
Gestation	64
Anatomy	65
Mating	65
Spit offs	67
Unpacking	67
Problem births	71
Crias	**75**
The newborn cria	75
Bottle feeding	76
Cria coats	78
The first few days	80
Weaning	80
Breeding for Colour	**83**
Showing Alpacas	**92**
Photographing your Alpacas	**94**
Visitors to the Paddock	**98**
Using the Fleece	**104**
Skirting	104
Washing	105
Carding	106
Spinning	106
Felting	110

INTRODUCTION

This book is designed for the alpaca owner with a small breeding herd, a growing herd or just a few pet males. It will also be of interest to someone who is thinking about buying alpacas. It aims to give a wide range of useful information to the new breeder or small herd owner but it is not a technical or veterinary manual, nor does it give in depth coverage on any particular topic. It cannot possibly answer every question that the new owner may ask, but it will answer some of them, and in addition, it will answer questions that the new owner didn't think to ask.

Outside South America the alpaca industry is relatively new, so keeping alpacas in a typical farm environment in Australasia, North America or Europe has a short history. We're learning as we go along. Much of the advice given in this book is opinion, based on experience – but with every year that goes by our experience grows and in some instances our opinions change. Also, what is standard practice in some parts of the world is unheard of in others. This book is written from a New Zealand perspective, and discusses practices common in New Zealand and Australia. American and European practices may differ. The animals however are the same worldwide – it is only the environment that changes. But the environment, to a large extent, will determine farming practices that work in different parts of the world.

Amongst other things this book will discuss some common health issues. I am a breeder, not a vet. You should always discuss any specific health issues with a veterinary professional.

And one last comment: the word "alpaca" is both singular and plural. One alpaca, many alpaca. (The same is also true for "cria".) However, it is natural for most people to use the plural "alpacas" when they are referring to more than one animal, and so throughout this book I have made a point of doing this.

Q: What's the difference between alpacas and llamas?

A: Alpacas are smaller, adults averaging 55-90Kg. They have spear shaped ears.
Llamas are bigger, adults averaging 130-200Kg. They have banana shaped ears.

BACKGROUND AND HISTORY

Background

Alpacas are *camelids*, closely related to llamas and also related to camels. Along with llamas, they are native to South America where over the last 500 years or so they have lived in the high altitudes of the Andes. As a result they have adapted to the thin air, extreme climate and intense sunlight of this mountainous region.

There are four distinct species of camelids native to South America – the alpaca, the llama, the guanaco and the vicuña. The alpaca and llama are domesticated; the guanaco and vicuña are wild. All these species can cross breed – and given the shortage of fences in the Andes it is likely that many of today's alpacas have at least some of their ancestry in llama, vicuña or guanaco herds.

The Dromedary camels of northern Africa and the Bactrian camels of central Asia are also camelids. They are known as the Old World camelids.

Camelids evolved in North America about 45 million years ago. For over 40 million years they were confined to that continent. Then two or three million years ago groups of camelids migrated away from North America, some moving west through Asia and others moving south to South America. Any remaining camelids in North America eventually became extinct, so ironically there are none native to that part of the world today.

There are varying theories about the modern ancestry of alpacas. Some people believe that they are descended from vicuñas, possibly bred thousands of years ago by native Indian populations of South America, while others believe that they evolved naturally as a separate species. Whichever answer is

> *Camelids evolved about 45 million years ago. There were once many species that are now extinct, ranging in size from the giant titanotyloptus (standing an impressive 3.5m at the shoulder), to the tiny rabbit sized protyloptus, which unlike modern camelids had four toes.*
>
> *Until about 3 million years ago North America and South America were not connected. Then the new land bridge of the Panama Isthmus appeared, which allowed animals to cross from one continent to the other. The isthmus was formed over millions of years by the collision of the Pacific and Caribbean tectonic plates and by the associated volcanic activity, creating islands which eventually joined up to form the isthmus. Camelids moved south across this new land bridge, eventually settling in the regions now known as Peru, Chile and Bolivia.*

correct, it is generally accepted that as a species they are more closely related to vicuñas than they are to llamas or guanacos.

Vicuñas are prized for their fleece and were hunted for this for many years, almost to the point of extinction. They are now a protected species in Peru and the harvesting of the fleece is carefully controlled. The staple length of the vicuña fleece is short, so they are shorn every two years. Vicuña fibre is the rarest and most valuable natural fibre in the world. The aim of alpaca breeders is to breed alpacas with fleeces that are just as desirable, but with greater density to the fleece, colour diversity and staple length.

There are two types of alpaca, differentiated by their fleece type. These are known as *huacaya* and *suri*. The huacaya is far more common than the suri and is the classic style of alpaca depicted in most artwork or advertising relating to alpacas; it has a fleece that protrudes outwards from the body at 90°, rather like a sheep's fleece, and has crimp like a sheep's fleece. The suri on the other hand has a silky fleece made up of individual locks which hang down from the body. The staple length of the suri is often longer than that of the huacaya. Huacaya and suri are considered to be the two *breeds* of alpaca. There may be slight differences of preferred head shape between the two breeds, but really it is the fleece style that differentiates them.

> **Crossing llamas with camels in Dubai**
>
> *Using artificial insemination, camel-llama hybrids have been bred at the Camel Reproduction Centre in Dubai, with the aim of producing an animal which has the strength and size of a camel combined with the temperament and wool production of a llama. These camel llama crosses are called "cama" and the first one was born in 1998. With a little human assistance, and despite the huge size difference between the two species, several perfectly healthy offspring have been born. Because camels and llamas have the same number of chromosomes it is expected that these offspring will be fertile and able to breed naturally themselves. It is easy to see that the more closely related species of alpacas and llamas, farmed by peasant communities on open land for hundreds of years, are likely to have cross bred quite frequently.*

History

When the Spaniards invaded Peru in the 1500's they brought their merino sheep with them, and commandeered the better grazing at the lower altitudes. This forced the native Indians into the Andean mountains with their alpacas. To this day most alpaca farming in Peru, Chile and Bolivia takes place in the mountains, with small herds being run by native Indian families who rely on their alpacas for clothing (fibre) and meat. By and large, breeding is not selective, and herd quality does not improve.

There are a few notable exceptions, predominantly in Peru. In these herds the quality of the alpacas has been improved, in some cases dramatically.

One of the most famous is the Accoyo herd, established by Don Julio Barreda. In 1948 with a herd of 500 alpacas he started breeding selectively, culling the inferior animals and using only the best males for breeding. Today many of the world's best alpacas have their ancestry in the Accoyo herd. Don Julio Barreda died in 2006 at the age of 87 having devoted a lifetime to improving the quality of alpacas.

The climate in the mountainous regions is harsh, with bitterly cold winter nights. The fleece of the huacaya alpaca protects the animal from the cold. The

suri is less fortunate, with its fleece parting along the spine exposing the backbone, and hanging close to the body, unable to trap much in the way of insulating warm air. The rainy months of the year are the summer months – December through to March, and this is when most cria are born. Suri cria born during the rainy months of the year have a much lower survival rate than huacaya cria born at the same time because the fleece does not offer as much protection. This probably explains why the suri is so much rarer than the huacaya – it has largely died out in the harsh mountain climate.

First imports

Apart from an experimental import of 84 alpacas into Australia in the 19th century, alpacas were first imported from South America into Australia, New Zealand and the USA in the late 1980's.

The original imports were from Chile, rather than Peru, and the alpacas were sourced primarily from peasant farmers.

Compared with more recent imports, the quality of most of these animals' fleeces was very poor. They tended to lack density and coverage so had low fleece weights. At that time Peru did not allow alpacas to be exported, so for breeders from Australasia and North America there were limited options. However, when Peru changed its laws and allowed exports to take place, breeders were able to select the best animals from Peruvian farms and as a result the herd quality in Australia, New Zealand and the USA began to improve rapidly.

Ruminants

The word "ruminant" comes from the Latin word *ruminare* which means "to chew over again". Cattle, sheep, deer and goats are true ruminants. They have a stomach that is divided into four compartments. Alpacas are modified ruminants. They also ruminate, but their stomachs are divided into just three compartments.

When an alpaca grazes it chews the grass sufficiently to be able to swallow it, and the grass then passes into the first compartment of the stomach. With the assistance of beneficial microbes in this compartment of the stomach (known as "C – 1") the fermentation process starts.

When an alpaca chews its cud it will bring a *bolus* of the food back up from C – 1 and chew it again in a figure of eight motion. Typically, the alpaca will chew up to 75 times and then swallow the cud, passing it into the next compartment of the stomach (C – 2) and bringing up another bolus to chew. If you watch a shorn alpaca chewing its cud you can see the chewed bolus moving down the long neck, and after a short pause you can see the new bolus coming back up.

The food further ferments in C – 2, again with the aid of beneficial microbes, and is then passed into the third compartment (C – 3) where stomach acids are produced to digest the food. Note that the microbes, which are still present in the food, will also be digested giving the alpaca its protein and important amino acids.

A sudden change in diet can affect the population of microbes in the gut, and this in turn affects the alpaca's health.

Life span

A commonly asked question is "How long do they live?" the usual answer is "About 20 years". Some live longer than that, some less. Remember that alpacas have not been farmed outside South America for much more than 20 years, so our records with these animals are themselves quite limited. The first imports from Chile were of unknown age. Their birth dates were all recorded as 01/01/1986. Our records start with the progeny of these first imports. There are births recorded in the registry to females who have reached 20 years of age, but the norm seems to be that they stop breeding before then.

Chewing cud

Huacaya alpaca

Suri alpaca

BEHAVIOUR

Alpaca behaviour

Alpacas are herd animals, and stress when separated from their herd. This is why you cannot have just one alpaca – the animal would be very lonely and unhappy. For the alpaca, there is security in numbers. If a new animal is introduced to an established herd it will immediately join them – even if it is unsure of its new paddock mates and so keeps to the outer edge of the group.

As with humans, alpacas have different personalities – some are shy and nervous while others are gregarious and brave. With the shy ones, the more exposure they have to humans, and the more pleasant this exposure is, the more likely they will be to begin to interact well with humans. The bold ones don't need a lot of encouragement! If you buy a couple of alpacas and they have had little human interaction you will need patience, but in time they will almost certainly come round.

Remember that alpacas are a prey animal, not a predator. At the back of their mind is always the thought that something might try to eat them. They are therefore understandably cautious and watchful of any potential predator, and that includes humans.

Alpacas don't like being grabbed. Because of this, they are constantly watching your arms. If you walk up to one, throwing your arms around in the air, the animal will probably move quickly off. If you keep your arms by your side, or behind your back, it will feel less threatened. Human instinct is to want to pat an alpaca, probably because the fleece looks so soft and tactile, but alpacas don't like being patted. Some will tolerate their necks or backs being touched, but it is a rare alpaca that will let you touch its head. And most alpacas don't like being touched around the tail.

Alpacas can kick! If anything or anyone brushes up behind them many have the instinctive reaction of kicking with a back leg. Whilst they have soft padded feet rather than hooves, a kick can still hurt.

Like camels, alpacas kush. First they "kneel down" by folding their front legs onto the ground, then they follow with their back legs, and then they wriggle into a comfortable position. Most of the time they kush with their front legs folded underneath them, but occasionally they stretch their legs out in front of them.

And yes, alpacas do spit. They rarely spit at humans; spitting is usually reserved for another alpaca that is annoying them. Some alpacas spit more than others. If the human is doing something particularly nasty to them (like shearing them, perhaps) a small percentage will spit. If you're shearing and you have a "spitty" alpaca, make sure you point the head away from yourself and the shearer, and any other human helpers – particularly if you would like them to come back and help again next year!

Spitting between alpacas usually starts as a minor argument. The first spit is often a warning, just a little mouthful of air, but a warning none the less. If the argument continues the spit will evolve into a spray of saliva, and after that it turns into real spitting - producing the notorious "green slime" that actually consists of party digested stomach contents. This spit smells particularly foul – if you get caught in the firing line you will be reminded of it until you can change your clothes. From the alpaca's point of view it must taste foul too because after the argument finishes both participants usually walk around with their bottom lips hanging down and green slime dribbling out. They will then often grab a mouthful of something astringent to chew, like penny royal or pine needles, to help combat the taste.

A very protective alpaca female with a new cria may spit at another alpaca or human that approaches her baby – if you have a female like this, and you need to attend to the cria, proceed with caution. I heard of one breeder who always took an umbrella with her when checking on any new cria of a particularly spitty dam!

There are times when you walk out into the paddock and it looks as if there's been a massacre. You find several alpacas are lying down, on their sides, sprawled out with their bellies to the sun. The fact is that alpacas like to sunbathe – more than just *like* to sunbathe, they *need* to sunbathe. They have a high requirement for vitamin D, and they can gain vitamin D by exposing their bellies to the sun.

It might be a good idea to warn your neighbours of this, otherwise when they first look out of the window and see an alpaca lying motionless in your paddock they will think it has died, and will rush over to tell you.

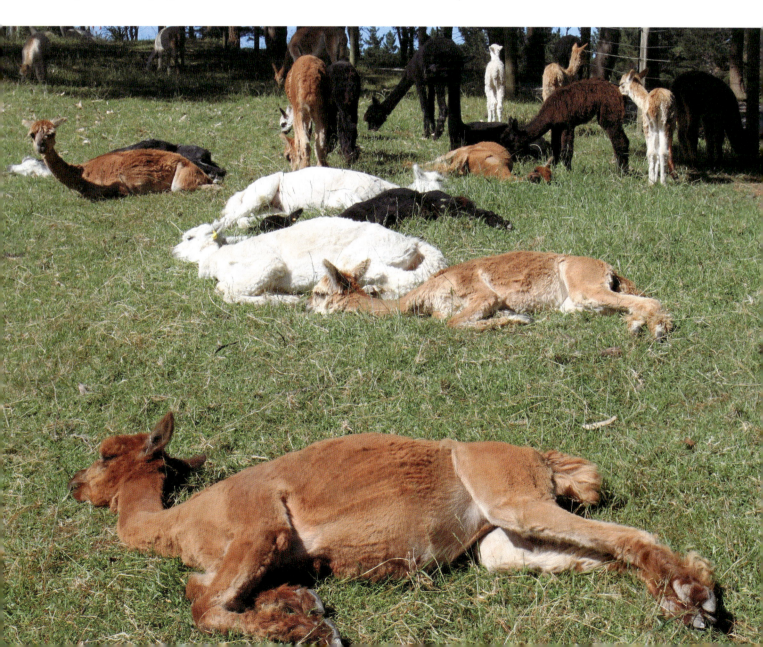

When they get hot, some alpacas like to cool down in water. If you have a pond or a dam in the paddock don't be surprised to find them wading around in it. When drinking from a trough they may soak their necks by resting their chins on the water. Some go further, and step in to the trough.

If you have a reticulated water system watch that this practice doesn't damage the float, or you may have an overflowing trough or one that doesn't fill properly.

Another method that alpacas use to help cool down is to kush with just their knees touching the ground, propping themselves up so that there is air flow underneath them. This helps to cool their bellies. Heavily pregnant females will often do this on a hot summer day.

Alpacas love to take a dust bath. They roll around vigorously on dry dusty soil, then shake themselves and walk off. If your paddocks don't have any bare patches when the alpacas move in to them they probably will when the alpacas move out. These *dust bath* areas tend to grow bigger the more they are used, and so on large alpaca farms you will often see a long bare streak on the grassy hillside. For the farmer, getting the grass to grow again can be a challenge because once there is a dust bath there the alpacas will keep on using it.

And on the topic of "bathroom" behaviour, alpacas use a communal dung pile. Boys tend to be tidier than girls. The dung pile in the males' paddock might be exactly that – a neat pile of dung. A tidy male will sniff the dung, step forward into exactly the right place, and drop the next deposit right on top of the last one.

But as with humans, some boys have tidier bathroom habits than others!

Dust bath

The dung pile in the girls' paddock will probably spread and become more of a dung area. When one female decides it's "toilet time" often others follow suit, and they stand in a line, so the bathroom keeps on getting bigger. Some farmers collect the dung, either daily or every few days, but many do not bother. The dung and urine fertilises the pasture in the dung area so dung areas tend to grow taller, greener grass.

The family cat can be a concern to your alpacas. When you look at your cat you see the adorable family pet that sits on your knee and purrs happily. The alpacas look at your cat and see a little brother of the puma that killed great grandma back in Peru. This is why they watch your cat carefully when he goes in to the paddock and may even follow him around. They want to make sure that he really is alone, and that he will leave them in peace.

The family dog is more of a worry, with good reason. Dog attacks on alpacas can be fatal. In New Zealand there are no foxes, and dogs are the only real killer from the animal kingdom. Alpacas know that dogs are killers and this is why they sound the alarm call when they see one.

In time they will get used to the resident dog on the farm, but will still watch it with caution.

People often ask if there are any behavioural differences between huacaya alpacas and suri alpacas. Some people think that suris are more skittish. On our farm we breed predominantly suris, but we also have some huacayas.

I have not noticed any difference in their behaviour – the "skittish" label probably arises from the fact that suris often have long fringes and can easily become "wool blind". If an alpaca can't see properly it will naturally be more cautious and jumpy. In my opinion suris with short fringes behave no differently from huacayas.

The puma (otherwise known as cougar, panther or mountain lion) is native to the Americas, and its range extends from Yukon in Canada to the southern Andes. It is genetically closer to the domestic cat than it is to lions and tigers.

It's not surprising therefore that alpacas are suspicious of your family cat!

> **Some basic rules to tell visitors to your alpaca paddock:**
>
> *Keep your arms close to your body – don't throw them around*
>
> *Walk at a steady pace, avoid sudden moves*
>
> *Don't chase the alpacas or try to grab them*
>
> *If the animal will let you touch it, touch its back or neck, not its head*
>
> *Remember alpacas can kick - don't brush up behind one unexpectedly*
>
> *Some mothers are very protective of their newborn cria, so keep an eye on mum if approaching her new baby*

Most herds have a leader, a few alpacas that would like to be the leader and a lot that are happy and confident with their place in the middle of the herd. Then there are some that everyone bosses around. These alpacas lack confidence generally and don't stand up for themselves. This is true whether it is a herd of males or females. If you are feeding a group of alpacas with supplements or treats and the herd leader takes a quick mouthful and then moves off to a bigger offering that you have just put out, few of the others will be brave enough to touch what she has left as this would risk incurring her wrath. They will sniff it, and move along.

Alpacas don't like being separated from the herd. If most of the herd moves off to the other side of the paddock they will all move off. If one alpaca isn't watching when the others move and is left behind, as soon as he finds the others have gone he will quickly look for them and run to join them. If you find one that is sitting down away from the others, and he doesn't jump up to join them when you approach, this alpaca might be sick. His condition needs to be investigated - see the health chapter in this book for some possible ailments.

This "sticking together as a herd" makes it easy for you to move a mob of alpacas because none of them want to be left behind. Be warned though that if you are trying to round them up and one makes a break and runs away the others will probably follow, so if you are moving a mob of alpacas don't let one peel off and run in the wrong direction.

If alpacas see danger – in the form of a dog, perhaps – they will sound the alarm call to warn the others. This alarm call is a shrill, repetitive call which can be heard from some distance. If you hear an alarm call and you observe the alpacas you will see them standing rigidly, staring in the same direction. Look where they are looking and you should be able to identify what they have seen.

> *I once heard the alarm call, and when I investigated I found that one of the stud boys was "crying wolf". The mob of females was on the move. As they passed the gate to his paddock, moving closer to a paddock of other boys, he decided to stop them in their tracks to keep them close to him. He pretended that he had noticed danger ahead and sounded the alarm call – so they all stopped, and turned to go back. His ploy had worked.*
>
> *Some of the other boys have also learned the trick. On occasions several of them sound the call together, but they are all staring in different directions and no-one has really seen anything. However, you can only cry wolf so many times before you are ignored, and now if a male sounds the call the females take little notice.*

The daily diary of an alpaca herd

First light – get up, stretch, move to preferred grazing place, graze for a while

Early morning – if the sun is warm sit and enjoy it, chew cud, maybe sunbathe a little

Mid morning – more grazing

Late morning – make way to preferred sitting area, maybe under tree, relax for a while, chew cud

Early afternoon – grazing again

Mid afternoon – enjoy more sunshine, chew cud, sit and relax

Late afternoon – grazing once more

Early evening – watch out for human servant with buckets of food, race to feeding area, scoff food provided

Dusk – bedtime

Communications

Alpacas communicate by humming. The hum can be an anxious hum, for instance when the animal is penned, "what are you going to do to me?" or when a mother is keeping an eye on her cria, "don't run off baby - come back!". It can be an annoyed hum ("this has taken too long, I want out NOW"), a distressed hum ("I'm lost"), a re-assuring hum ("it's OK, I'm here, baby"), a pleading hum ("Mum! Get up, I'm hungry") or a fed up "humph!". When a cria has just been born the mother will hum to it and the cria will hum back. This is really a conversational hum and its use decreases as the cria grows. Females will also "cluck" to their crias, and before long the crias will start to cluck back.

The alarm call is sounded if an alpaca sees potential danger and it warns the rest of the herd to be careful.

When seducing a female, the male *orgles*. He is singing her a love song! Different males have different voices, and, combined with varying confidence levels in their amorous approaches, the girls find some sexier than others. The girls prefer a strong confident approach to a hesitant wimpy one!

Throughout the act of mating the male continues to orgle - this often causes any empty females within earshot to get excited, and they come and sit nearby awaiting their turn.

When males are fighting they screech – they are effectively screaming loudly and yelling abuse at each other.

Communication is also made through ear positions - upright ears show the animal is alert, ears slightly back show the animal is relaxed, and ears right back show anxiety.

Body positions give a message to other alpacas. Females may pose for the male, the pose might say "Look at me, aren't I beautiful, wouldn't you like to make love to me?" or it might say the opposite: "I'm big and strong so don't even think about it buster, I'm already pregnant!". When trying to interpret this body language to confirm pregnancy status the two poses can look very similar and be quite confusing.

If one alpaca warns another to keep her distance she may raise her head as if she is about to spit. The fact is, if the other alpaca doesn't back down, she probably will spit. If the second alpaca refuses to be dictated to by the first one she may well raise her head too, warning of her own intention to spit. There may now be an argument between the two as neither wants to give in. This is really an argument about dominance between herd members. A submissive alpaca will always give in to a dominant one, unless perhaps the dominant one is threatening her baby, in which case she might be braver than usual in order to protect the cria.

Moving your alpacas

Alpacas are generally easy to move from one paddock to another. Often they will come when called, especially if they are keen to move to better pasture, or are curious and want to know what's going on.

Rattling a bucket of pellets usually has the desired effect and they will come running.

If neither of these work, a "moving fence" might be the answer. A highly visible rope or tape, held between two people, serves as a barrier and the people can move it as necessary to direct the alpacas. The easiest solution here it to walk the alpacas to a fixed fence line, then move the rope behind them, encouraging them to follow the fence to the desired gate or location.

If alpacas are to be transported any distance they can travel in a float, trailer, van, truck or utility vehicle. Halter trained alpacas will walk in to most vehicles or trailers which are high enough for them to stand in. Unless a suitable yard, or loading area and ramp, is available which funnels the alpaca in to the vehicle, non halter trained alpacas will probably need to be lifted in.

The easiest way to do this is for two people to lift the front legs and fold them as if in a kush position while the alpaca still has its back feet on the ground. The front of the alpaca can now be slid onto the floor of the vehicle. If the alpaca does not voluntarily lift its back legs and step in to the vehicle, the back can be easily lifted and pushed in – the back half of the animal is much lighter in weight and more manoeuvrable than the front half.

Halter training

Halter training of alpacas is best carried out when the animal is young although older ones can also be successfully halter trained. Some take to the halter easily, walking happily on a lead after just one or two sessions. Most though take a while to get used to the idea. A halter trained alpaca is easier to move around the farm, and load into a vehicle, than a non-halter trained one. Halter trained alpacas are also easier to work with when handling – i.e. worming, inoculating, trimming toenails etc.

How do you halter train an alpaca?

Obviously, to start with you need a halter and a lead. The halter must fit properly or the alpaca will be uncomfortable – and uncomfortable alpacas don't co-operate. The golden rule when fitting a halter is that the noseband must fit correctly and be positioned so as not to obstruct the airways. This means that the noseband

a well fitting halter

sits up quite high on the nose, close to the eye sockets. If you feel along the top of an alpaca's nose you will notice that there is soft cartilage close to the nostrils, and it becomes bone further up. The halter must fit on to the bony part, not the cartilage, or it will interfere with the alpaca's breathing.

An adjustable halter is a good idea, where both the noseband and the neck strap can be altered to fit the alpaca perfectly. This means that one halter can be used for several alpacas and, within the limits of the halter's size, can be adjusted as the alpacas grow.

In order to catch your alpaca and put the halter on you will need a confined space. See the section on yards and pens starting on page 32 in this book.

There are differing views on how halter training should be carried out. If you talk to local breeders you will probably hear a variety of methods that are used. The method you choose to use will depend on the time you have available and what appeals to you most.

Rightly or wrongly, here are my views on halter training:

Halter training is best undertaken in a series of short sessions. The number of sessions, and the progress made during each session, depends largely on the response of the alpaca in question. The first session might just be putting the halter on and then taking it off again, so that the alpaca learns that even though this was a very odd experience nothing nasty happened.

The next step is to encourage the alpaca to walk beside you with the halter on. What you do now will probably depend on the reaction of the alpaca. If he walks hesitantly you can walk slowly alongside, encouraging him to follow your direction. When you feel you've made some progress, no matter how small, take the halter off, praise the alpaca for doing well, and release him.

Alpacas like this usually "get it" quite quickly. Try to finish on a good note, when the alpaca is co-operating, and release him on your terms - not his. This means that if the alpaca is desperately trying to get away from you, pulling frantically, you should hold him until he has calmed down, then slowly release him. In an ideal world you would remove the halter and he would still be standing there calmly while you back off.

Unfortunately it is not an ideal world, and some alpacas are a challenge to halter train. Here are some common reactions that you might have to deal with:

Scenario 1. *Frantic attempts to escape, throwing himself in the air, jumping, pulling in all directions. Great! This alpaca is moving, he just needs to calm down and move where you want him to, not where he wants to. Your main concern will be that he might injure himself when he lands awkwardly. Alpacas like this are best trained on a soft surface, like grass, rather than on concrete. You just need patience. In the end he will give up on his antics and take a sensible step forward. Call it a day at this point, praise him for doing the right thing, and release him.*

Scenario 2. *Putting on the brakes, refusing to move. Again, great! This alpaca is not panicking or being silly, he is just cautious or suspicious. Here you may have to either stand in front of him, gently pulling on the lead until he moves, or stand beside him with your hand on his rump, encouraging him to move. Once he has taken a few hesitant steps praise him and finish the session.*

Scenario 3. *Chin on the ground and not moving – trickier! You need patience. An alpaca will only stand with his chin on the ground for so long – in the end he will lift his head. You might like to finish at this point, while he is upright – reward him for standing nicely by letting him go. Tomorrow is another day – maybe tomorrow, maybe in a few days, you will get to scenario 2 above and be able to move on from there.*

Scenario 4. *Sitting down – this can also be tricky. You need to stand him up if he won't stand by himself. This is best achieved by putting your fingers under his rump, beneath his tail – he won't like this and he should stand. If he's prepared to tolerate this you might need to exert a little more pressure and physically lift his rear end so his legs are more or less straight. At this point you have to hope that his front end will follow and he will stand up. If he doesn't, and just settles back down again, it's back to square 1. Sooner or later he will stand and then you're into scenario 2 above. Often in cases like this the hesitant walking will be punctuated by frequent sitting down. If that happens, end the session while he's standing, or preferably, walking – don't finish a* session while he's kushed.

Scenario 5. Lying down – this can be a challenge, especially if he lies defiantly on his side. Roll him in to the kush position, then proceed as for scenario 4 above.

Even the worst students seem to get it eventually; it just requires persistence on the part of the human.

Halter training is worth the effort. Well trained alpacas walk happily on a lead, even in unfamiliar locations, and are a joy to work with.

THE FARM ENVIRONMENT

Stocking ratio

Your farm's stocking ratio depends entirely on the quality and volume of pasture that it grows. If you live in the arid outback of Australia the stocking ratio on your farm will be quite different from that on a farm situated in the lush pasturelands of the Waikato. It also depends on whether your alpaca herd consists of pregnant females who are also nursing young cria, or of neutered males who have nothing to do all day but eat and get fat. Alpacas are very efficient converters of feed, and it is believed that per head they eat less than sheep. So as a general guide if you could run 10 sheep in your paddocks you can probably run 10 alpacas.

Fences

Generally alpacas don't challenge fences. If suitably motivated they can jump over standard height farm fences, but usually they don't.

Motivation to jump over a fence could include a range of factors. Firstly, fear - for instance, the desire to escape from an aggressive paddock mate or some other perceived danger. Secondly, during weaning or other separation, where the separated alpaca wants to re-join the herd. It's amazing how high a determined cria can jump if mum is on the other side. And thirdly there's that age old desire for sex! A suitably aroused male can easily jump – or fall, while standing on his hind legs propositioning the girls on the other side – over the fence to get to welcoming females. If he does this you will know it's happened as he will stay with the females and you will find him there. However, if the female jumps the fence in order to be mated, she will probably jump back again when finished to return to her cria or the rest of her herd. In this case you probably won't know what has happened – and eleven and a half months later you wonder where that cria came from!

The easiest solution to the fencing question for alpacas is just to use standard 7 or 9 wire farm fences, with the bottom wires close enough to the ground to stop a cria from getting through. Standard fences range from 1.05 to 1.2 metres high. Most farms or lifestyle blocks will have this sort of fencing. 1.8 metre high deer fencing is not required for alpacas. However, if you have standard height fences - and entire males and open females on the farm - it is a good idea to make sure there are at least two fences between them. This discourages the girls from flirting with the boys and getting them excited.

Barbed wire is not a good fencing material for alpacas because alpacas tend to stick their heads through fences. Barbs on the wire can get caught in their fleece, or worse, cause injury to the alpaca. If you have sheep or deer netting, and the spaces are large enough

Panama's story:

I did my usual "head count" one morning and discovered that one of the young females, Panama, was missing. I went looking for her and found her completely entangled in electric tape that had been strung around some olive trees in the paddock. (It wasn't connected to any power supply, so it wasn't "live".) The more she had struggled to escape, the tighter the tape became. Fortunately the tape wasn't tight around the front of her neck because her legs were caught in it and had crossed under her chin, and I was able to untangle her. Once she was free she managed to sit up, then she staggered to her feet and groggily walked off.

Not content with this one adventure, some months later Panama got herself caught in a nine wire fence at the bottom of a hill. She must have kushed, then rolled on her side and her two lower legs had slid under the bottom wire, with her two upper legs going through the fence a couple of wires up.

Panama has always been a greedy soul, and has big solid thighs, one of which was firmly pinned in place under the bottom wire. I assume that as she struggled to extract herself she had slid further down the hill, until her chest came to rest against the fence. From this position she couldn't roll back to kush, so she couldn't stand. I had to ease this heavy-weight alpaca out of her predicament without touching the electric wire at the top of the fence! Once she got her balance back she was able to stand and was none the worse for wear, except for a little chaffing on her ample thigh.

Panama, some years later

for alpacas to get their heads through, keep a regular eye on the herd. This sort of netting is made by looping or twisting the wires together to hold them in place where they cross over, and long fleece can get caught in these loops, trapping the animal in the fence. If you have post and rail fences designed for larger animals (like horses) make sure the spaces between the rails are small enough to contain alpacas – you may need to run a wire between the rails to reduce the size of the gap.

If you use electric tape, be careful. Many alpacas have strangled themselves in electric tape - usually when it is use in a temporary fence (and often when it hasn't been hooked up the current), but also when it has been left rolled up in the paddock.

Electric fencing is not generally very effective with alpacas (unless it is combined with a standard 7 or 9 wire farm fence). This is probably because of the insulating properties of the fleece. A two wire electric fence that is suitable for cattle will not contain alpacas! Alpacas can walk under an electric wire without seeming to notice that there is current running through it.

Yards and pens

When you want to work with your alpacas, for instance when giving injections or when halter training, you will need to pen them. Pens do not have to be elaborate, but if you are building pens from scratch you can create an ideal shape and size which will work well for you and make handling your alpacas much easier.

Firstly, consider where you will place the pen. In deciding this, you will have to consider how you will get the alpacas to actually go into the pen. A pen in the middle of a paddock would be unlikely to work because the alpacas could not be funnelled in to it. Pens are best situated beside some sort of farm race or yard area. The alpacas can be moved into the race or yard, and funnelled in to the pen from there. If your farm does not have a suitable race or yard area you can create a capture point in a corner of a paddock, preferably where it can be easily accessed from other paddocks.

Secondly, consider the design of the pen itself. An ideal pen for alpacas would have sides around 2m long, and would be high enough to prevent them from jumping out– so 1.2m is a good height. You can purpose build a pen of this size using fence posts rammed or concreted into the ground and pen walls made from fencing timber; remember that it needs to be strong enough to withstand an alpaca's kick. If you don't want to build a permanent structure you can improvise, using four farm gates, panels of swimming pool fence, heavy mesh panels or whatever you can lay your hands on that will create an appropriately sized pen.

Most people build their pens from heavy fencing timber or other similarly treated outdoor timber. Remember however that rough sawn timber rails can cause splinters if you grab one from the wrong angle!

If the pen is too big you will find it difficult to catch the alpacas once they're in it, if it is too small you will have problems getting them to go in, especially if you want to put several in the pen together.

These days there are portable aluminium yards and pens available, which come in either "sheep" or "alpaca" heights and lock together at the corners using long pins. They are easy to relocate if you change your mind about where to put them, and you can open any side to let animals in or out.

Shelter

Alpacas have evolved in a harsh climate and can cope with quite low temperatures. They don't need to be housed at night, or even in winter unless the

climate is extreme (there may be parts of Europe where farm animals are traditionally housed in winter and alpaca husbandry will follow suit) but in New Zealand healthy alpacas spend their lives in the paddock. However, like all livestock, alpacas appreciate shade on hot summer days, especially if they are still in full fleece. Big trees are ideal for providing shade; alpacas like to sit under trees and often choose to sleep there at night. If your paddock doesn't have trees you should provide some sort of shade structure for them. If you have two adjoining paddocks and neither has shade, consider building a shade structure straddling the fence line which can be accessed from either paddock.

Shade structures can be robust shed-like structures built from permanent materials with roofs of iron, other commonly used roofing material or plywood, or they can be constructed using a centre pole or poles, and stretching shade cloth or shade sails from them.

A good long term solution is to plant trees. Some trees grow very fast and are available in large sizes from a garden centre or specialist tree nursery. Ask advice from the nursery as to which species will grow quickly in your area. Planting fast growing trees will provide adequate shade fairly quickly if you have just a few alpacas. In most parts of New Zealand poplars and willows can be cheaply grown by sticking "poles" or "stakes" in the ground. They form roots quickly if the ground is moist enough and become sizeable trees within a year or two. Alpacas aren't hard on trees like cattle, nor do they ring bark trees like horses do.

However, some protection for newly planted trees is a good idea as alpacas will eat the leaves as high as they can reach – and with their long necks, that is quite high.

Poisonous trees and plants

Generally farmers don't plant poisonous trees on farms, especially in paddocks where animals could reach them. However, people do plant ornamental trees in gardens, including farm gardens, and along driveways, and these may well include poisonous ones. Two of the most poisonous are oleander and rhododendron (including the smaller species related to rhododendron, azalea). Both these trees are beautiful, with lovely flowers, and both extremely poisonous.

Oleander comes in a variety of colours, from pink through apricot shades to white. Rhododendrons come in a huge array of vibrant colours and include the tropical variety, *vireya*.

Other poisonous trees include yew, cestrum and laburnum. Box hedging is also poisonous.

In New Zealand, the native shrub tutu (generally found in patches of native bush) is highly toxic. It is reported that in 1870 tutu killed a circus elephant in Otago. The elephant was grazing in long grass where young tutu shoots were also growing. Tutu leaves are quite distinctive, with three to five parallel veins running from the stem to the tip.

At certain times of the year oak leaves can be poisonous, but most people agree that the animals would have to eat them in volume to be affected.

Macrocarpa is a common tree on farms and many people believe that it causes abortions, the same may be true of pine needles if eaten in volume. However there are mixed opinions on these theories and more research is needed, especially in relation to alpacas.

Some paddock weeds are also toxic, with ragwort being one of the more dangerous.

In most cases alpacas would need to have prolonged exposure to poisonous weeds to be seriously affected. However, it is a good idea to check your paddocks and remove any potentially harmful plants.

Local vets are usually a good resource when it comes to poisonous plants. If you don't know what you have growing on your farm, ask the vet to have a look. He or she may not know the names of all the plants, but should know if any are poisonous.

Annoying plants and fleece contamination

Some plants are particularly good at getting entangled in fleeces. Dock is a prime example. The reddish brown seed heads and stalks get entangled in fleeces regularly (especially suri fleeces) if dock plants are allowed to grow to maturity.

Thistles – particularly the scotch thistle – are another curse because the leaves and seed heads can get caught in the fleece where they are a challenge for human fingers to remove.

Brambles, gorse and other spiky leaved plants can cause similar problems.

Pine trees drop needles and other debris – the needles aren't difficult to remove, they are just a nuisance. There are many other trees with serrated or spiky leaves or seedheads, or twigs with rough bark, which are also annoying.

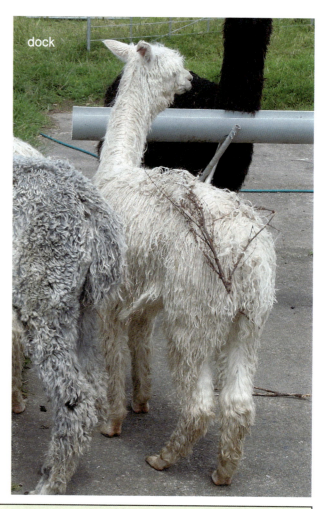

I sold five strong healthy males to a couple who were well prepared for them. Their fencing was secure, and before delivering the boys I walked through their paddocks with them, checking for poisonous weeds. We didn't find any. I gave them my "new owners" handout which included a list of common poisonous plants.

The boys moved in to their new home, and the couple rang me from time to time to give me progress reports on how they were doing. Clearly these people adored their alpacas and cared for them well.

They rang me one day and I asked how the boys were. "We just buried two of them" they said "and another two are really sick and we think they'll die too." They explained what had happened. An ornamental tree in their garden had blocked their view of the paddock and so they had decided to chop it down. After chopping it down they threw the trunk and branches onto the bonfire in the paddock to burn later, and didn't think any more of it. When they found two of the boys lying dead in the paddock, and two more looking very sick, they were shocked. The vet who attended the sick animals thought they had been poisoned and identified the tree on the bonfire as oleander. I said "But don't you remember, oleander was at the top of the list of poisonous plants that I gave you!" and they said "Yes, but we didn't know what oleander was."

In the end one more alpaca died, but the fourth one recovered. It appears that the fifth boy hadn't eaten any of the leaves as he showed no symptoms of having been poisoned.

Both oleander and rhododendron can be lethal. That is why I have included photos of them in this book!

3 Tips for handling alpacas by yourself:

Tip #1—catching and holding the animal by yourself:

Use a small catch pen, no more than 2m x 2m—the alpaca will be easy to catch and you can wedge him between yourself and the wall in one of the corners

Tip #2 - giving an injection by yourself:

Hold the alpaca by placing his neck under your arm, with his head pointing backwards behind you. You can firmly grip the alpaca this way while still keeping both hands free to give the injection. And if he spits, you're out of the firing line!

Tip #3 - oral drenching by yourself:

Use a purpose made syringe with a long metal nozzle rather than an ordinary plastic syringe designed for use with a needle. The long nozzle slips easily between the teeth and the cheek, so the alpaca receives the drench at the back of the mouth and has little option but to swallow it.

A cheap and easy alpaca feeder:

Use a length of plastic guttering nailed to the fence as an alpaca feeder. Guttering is about the right size for alpacas to feed from and the greedy one can't be at both ends at once.

For portable feeders put the guttering on legs, or instead of guttering use large plastic pipes cut in half lengthwise. You can lay the guttering or pipe straight on the ground if it is well balanced and you don't have small animals or birds around (like ducks) that will steal the food from it.

HEALTH

Generally alpacas enjoy good health. They need to be shorn once a year or they will suffer from the heat in summer, but health-wise, they don't require a lot of input from humans. Their tails are naturally short and don't need docking. In most parts of the world they don't get fly strike (although there are occasional reports of this). They don't get foot rot or laminitis. They usually have problem free pregnancies followed by easy births.

There are however a few things you can do to help them maintain good health. There are also some things that you can look out for that might point to a developing problem, which if identified early enough can be successfully treated. These will be discussed in this chapter.

There may be some location specific conditions as well that could affect alpacas in your area, you should talk to your vet and make local enquiries as to what (if any) these might be.

Body scoring

Alpacas should not be fat, nor should they be skin and bone. But like humans, they vary. Some remain skinny no matter what they eat and others can't seem to lose weight even when on a very restricted diet.

However as a general rule huacaya alpacas should measure "3" on the body scoring chart below, which depicts a cross section of the spine just behind the shoulders. You should feel the alpaca's back at this point with your hand – don't rely on a visual check because thick fleeces can disguise the condition underneath.

Suri alpacas should carry more fat on the back than huacayas, so a body score of "3" for a suri is considered thin. With their fleece parting at the backbone the suri needs more fat at that point to protect the animal from the cold.

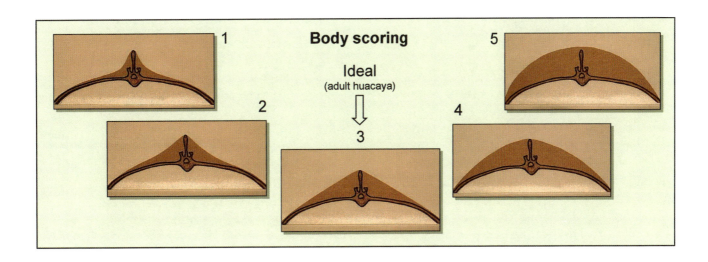

Other places to check your alpaca's body condition are the thighs and chest. The thighs should look firmly muscled. They should not be fat, almost touching each other as the animal walks, nor should they be thin and wasted with a lot of space between them.

The chest should join the front legs more or less at right angles and create a straight line between the legs. A round flabby chest points to an obese animal whereas a hard bony "V" shaped chest might indicate that the animal is emaciated.

Bear in mind when using the body scoring chart on the previous page that, like suris, crias should have more fat on their backs than adults, and that the chart has been designed for use with adult huacayas.

Worming

As with all livestock, alpacas can be affected by parasitic worms. Stomach worms, tapeworms, lung worms, coccidia and liver fluke have all been reported in alpacas. Most alpacas go through life without any obvious problems caused by any of these, but prevention is better than cure.

Many alpaca owners routinely worm their animals two or three times a year, using a wormer that kills stomach worms and, depending on the active ingredients contained in the drench, may also kill tapeworm, liver fluke and lung worms.

It is not usual for any of the common wormers to kill coccidia but if your vet

diagnoses this he or she can provide you with a wormer specifically for this parasite.

If your alpaca herd consists of a few tidy boys with good toilet habits and neat dung piles, and your property was previously grazed by cattle or horses (i.e. not sheep or other camelids) – and you have plenty of grazing for your animals, then worms will probably not be an issue for you. The life cycle of the parasitic worm is to shed eggs inside the host (in our case, an alpaca) so the eggs will be expelled in the faeces. Once on the ground the eggs hatch and the hatchlings wait in the pasture for another host to ingest them.

If your alpacas have a tidy dung pile and they don't graze on or adjacent to it, then they will not ingest any newly hatched worms. However, if you have a large herd of females (with untidy toilet habits) and insufficient grazing, then the alpacas will be forced to graze the lush grass growing in the expansive dung areas, so the risk of re-infection is much greater.

Rather than routinely worming their herds, some farmers prefer to carry out faecal egg counts and only worm the animals when necessary. To carry out a faecal egg count a small fresh faecal sample is collected from a specific animal and is mixed into a thick sugar or saline solution and placed in a test tube. Any eggs in the faeces will slowly float to the surface of the dense liquid and from there a drop of the solution can be inspected under the microscope; this process can be sped up by spinning the sample in a centrifuge. If the sample that is collected is too old, or it is kept too long before testing, any eggs that it originally contained may have already hatched (with the hatchlings then having climbed out of the faeces), giving an inaccurate result.

Broadband (born on the day that our broadband was finally connected)

Broadband's story:

Some years ago we had a young male, Broadband, that became increasingly thin, to the point that he was almost skin and bone. He wasn't "down", he moved with the herd, but he just didn't graze. Faecal samples showed no parasites (although there were almost no faeces to sample as there was no food going through his system). I called the vet. He listened to his heart and breathing and took his temperature then shook his head and said "I really don't know what's wrong with him". He wasn't anaemic. His heart was fine. His breathing was normal. He had no temperature. The vet took blood samples, they showed nothing abnormal. I decided to worm him for tapeworm even though there were no signs of this.

The next day he started grazing happily again. Of course it may just have been a coincidence.

My (very non-scientific) theory is that if his stomach was full of tapeworm it would have felt full, and so he wouldn't have been hungry and therefore didn't bother to graze. When the tapeworm was gone his stomach was empty and he felt hungry so he started eating again.

I told the vet what I had done, and what had happened the next day. I said "But you vets always say that tapeworm doesn't hurt them". He said "Well, that's what we were told at university – but actually back in the 'angora goat' days I did see several goats that died from it".

In the warm humid northern parts of New Zealand a notable parasitic worm is the *haemonchus contortus*, or barbers pole worm. This worm sucks blood from the host and a large infestation can cause rapid anaemia which in turn leads to weakness, lethargy and, if untreated, death.

Signs that the owner may notice in an alpaca affected by barbers pole worm include loss of condition, lethargy and anaemia. If an animal is lethargic it will be relatively easy to catch and check for anaemia. Ask your vet to show you how to check the inner eyelids for this – the inner eyelids should be quite pink regardless of the skin colour of the alpaca, but in an anaemic alpaca they will be pale, and if the animal is badly anaemic they can become almost white. Urgent attention is needed in such cases; ask your vet for advice.

Coccidia can also be detected in a faecal egg count, if this is found your vet can prescribe an appropriate wormer. With most strains of coccidia animals carrying a high burden will show signs of ill thrift. There is one strain that is more serious than the others, commonly called E Mac (*eimeria macusaniensis*). The eggs of E Mac are much larger than other coccidia and shaped rather like a miniature avocado. A high burden of E Mac can be fatal in young cria or susceptible adults so if detected in a faecal egg count it must be dealt with quickly.

Tapeworm is best diagnosed by inspecting the faeces for tapeworm segments. These can appear as single white segments, or as long strands of worm. Eggs may or may not show in a faecal sample. Whilst tapeworm itself does not usually cause serious problems I believe that in extreme cases it can cause ill thrift. If you worm an alpaca for tapeworm, and you are able to find the faeces passed by the animal after worming, you may be surprised at the volume of worm that appears.

Wormers can be administered orally or by injection. (Currently "pour-ons" do not work with alpacas.) Take your vet's advice as to dosages, and don't be surprised if you are advised to exceed the sheep dose rate by 50%.

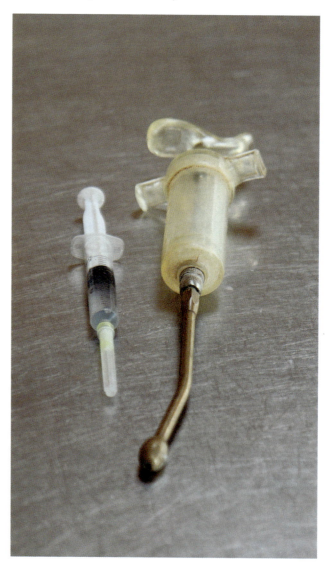

Toenail trimming

Alpaca toenails are rather like extra strong human toenails in their composition. That is, they are not hard hooves or claws, but a nail that covers the toe.

White alpacas usually have pink feet and light coloured nails (but not always – some have dark feet), and black and coloured alpacas usually have dark feet and dark nails.

For some reason the dark and light coloured nails grow differently, with white nails seeming to grow faster and longer, often becoming quite curled if not trimmed, whereas the black ones seem to grow straighter and need less trimming. I suspect that the pigment in dark nails makes them more brittle and as well as growing more slowly they break off or wear down more easily. They don't need trimming very often, if at all, while the lighter ones are more pliable and grow faster, and may need to be trimmed several times a year.

Toenails are usually trimmed with sharp pointed clippers. Before cutting in to the nail, check where the toe is. If the nails are long the toes may have grown into them more than you realise, and you could cut the alpaca's toes as well if not careful.

First of all look under the foot, and using the pointed tip of the clippers dig any mud out from inside the toenail, so you can see where the toe finishes. Then you can start cutting. There are a variety of techniques, but an easy solution is to cut the tip off the nail, then trim each side into a natural shape. If in doubt, make small cuts!

Overly long teeth

Teeth

If you look at an alpaca's mouth you will see that there are front teeth on the bottom jaw, but not at the top. These are the teeth that the alpaca uses to cut grass and other plants when grazing. The teeth should line up with the dental pad above to allow for efficient feeding. The teeth continue to grow and when they do line up properly are usually kept at the right length through constant use. However, sometimes they protrude in front of the dental pad so there is nothing to check the growth, and then they get too long. Your vet can trim them if required (although some experienced breeders do it themselves). Teeth can be cut using a wire cutter, or a small rotary cutting tool.

After the teeth have been trimmed they often function correctly and may never need to be touched again.

At the back of the mouth alpacas have upper and lower molars for chewing. The word "molar" comes from the Latin word *mola* which means millstone – and that is exactly what these teeth are. Alpaca molars are much sharper than your own molars, which in humans are quite rounded. If for any reason you need to feel inside your alpaca's mouth, remember not to place your finger between the upper and lower molars or you could be severely chewed!

All males, and some females, grow fighting teeth. The purpose of these teeth is obvious from the name – they are sharp, needle like teeth and they can cause injury to fellow alpacas if allowed to grow long. These should also be trimmed and your vet can do this.

Again, some breeders will handle this job themselves, using the same tooth cutting tools or possibly dog nail clippers. Be careful with dog nail clippers as they can cause the tooth to fracture.

Vitamin D and rickets

Having evolved at high altitudes in the Andes, alpacas have adapted to the intense sunlight associated with this climate. In all mammals, ultraviolet light is absorbed into the skin and is converted by the body into vitamin D3. Insufficient ultraviolet light causes vitamin D3 deficiency which in turn causes rickets and other painful bone diseases. Alpacas in the Andes obtain sufficient sunlight to make the amount of vitamin D3 that they require, but outside that environment vitamin D3 needs to be artificially administered. It is available in injectable form, usually in a combination injection of vitamins A, D3 and E.

Remember that the aim of the injection is to provide adequate vitamin D3, not to overdose the alpaca on vitamin A, so check that the ratio of A to D3 is appropriate in the product you use. For example, in New Zealand there are two commonly available A, D and E cocktails that come from the same laboratory. However, each mix has quite different ratios of the vitamins A and D3. One contains 60,000 international units of vitamin A and 500,000 international units of D3, while the other contains 500,000 international units of vitamin A and only 75,000 international units of D3. If you were to use the second of these products, in order to give your alpacas the appropriate amounts of vitamin D3 there would be a serious risk of overdosing vitamin A.

Like alpacas, humans are also mammals that require vitamin D3. If you think about humans, dark skinned people have evolved in the tropics where there is ample intense sunlight. The dark pigment in their skin protects them from the adverse effects of too much sun. Fair skinned people have evolved in the temperate zones where there are fewer hours of sunlight, and what sunlight there is, is less intense. If a fair skinned Norwegian girl moves to central Africa her skin will burn in the harsh sunlight, but she will have no shortage of vitamin D3. If a dark skinned African girl moves to Norway she will be at risk of vitamin D3 deficiency because her dark skin will block what little ultraviolet light there is. The same is true with alpacas. Dark skinned alpacas are able to absorb less ultraviolet light than pink skinned alpacas, so black alpacas are at greater risk than white alpacas of going down with rickets.

Heavily fleeced alpacas, with coverage over the face, under the belly and down to the feet, have less bare skin to expose to the sun than do poorly covered, thin fleeced alpacas. Unshorn alpacas, especially in summer, are less able to make vitamin D3 than their shorn paddock mates. Sunlight is also absorbed through the eyes, so if the fleece covers the eyes the alpaca will absorb less sunlight. Therefore, the more fleece on the animal, and the darker the animal, the more the demand for artificial vitamin D3.

Young, growing alpacas and pregnant females with a growing foetus require plenty of vitamin D3 to form strong bones.

Symptoms and treatment of rickets/vitamin D (or phosphate) deficiency

Symptoms of rickets vary, but all are associated with painful or weak bones.

If a cria suddenly becomes knock kneed (and when it happens it really is sudden), suspect rickets. An alpaca walking with an awkward gait, a hunch-backed alpaca with an "S" shaped neck, or an alpaca that chooses to sit down a lot (and then walks stiffly when it moves) may be suffering from rickets. In most cases a vitamin D3 shot will rectify the situation quite quickly and the symptoms will disappear within days.

Many breeders are now supplementing all their alpacas with vitamin D3 several times a year.

Talk to your vet about the products available in your area and the recommended frequency and dose rates for your alpacas.

Ryegrass staggers

Many years ago, ryegrass in New Zealand was infected with an endophyte to combat the Argentine stem weevil. This endophyte is a fungus that protects the grass from being eaten by the weevil, but the fungus produces *mycotoxins* which cause ryegrass staggers.

The toxins affect the brain and central nervous system of the animal and this is what causes it to stagger when walking. The toxins are mostly produced in summer and autumn, when the fungus is active, so ryegrass staggers is usually seen at this time of year.

The endophyte is more concentrated in the plant in the seed heads and at the base of the stem. A susceptible alpaca is less likely to be affected when eating ryegrass leaves than when eating the seed heads and stalks. Consequently, if your pasture is overgrazed in summer and consists mainly of seed heads and stalks, with very little leaf content, staggers is more likely to be a problem.

These days ryegrass is available with different entophytes that do not cause staggers. However, it is impossible to tell the species apart by looking at them, and most pastures were planted before these new grasses became available, so most ryegrass pasture in New Zealand has the potential to cause ryegrass staggers. Even if you were to spray out the old ryegrass and replace it with a new variety, the older grass is likely to re-establish itself through the pasture and you would not know which grass plants were safe and which were toxic.

Symptoms of ryegrass staggers

The first noticeable symptom is a slight tremor in the head and neck, and as the disease advances this tremor becomes worse. It progresses into an obvious swaying of the head, followed by an unstable, staggery gait, hence the name "ryegrass staggers". A badly affected animal will have trouble standing and may fall down.

Treatment of ryegrass staggers

Only a small percentage of alpacas are susceptible to ryegrass staggers. Most do not seem to be affected, but if a young alpaca shows any symptoms you should move the affected animal off the ryegrass so that it can recover. If it does not recover at a young age it is likely to be affected for life.

Sunburned nose

If you move an animal off affected pasture and you opt to feed hay, the hay should be from grass other than ryegrass. The toxins in the grass can remain active even after the grass has been turned into hay.

Magnesium deficiency *can cause similar symptoms to ryegrass staggers. There are several causes of magnesium deficiency, including an imbalance of calcium and magnesium in feed and the use of potassium based fertilisers on the pasture. Magnesium is easy to supplement and commonly available at stock food stores.*

PEM *and* ***vitamin D3 deficiency*** *are other conditions that can cause staggering.*

Skin conditions

In warm, humid climates some alpacas can develop **fungal infections**, which usually manifest themselves as crusty growths on the surface of the skin (often on the tips of the ears) or sometimes as bare patches of skin. Your vet can provide you with a suitable fungicidal ointment to combat this.

Mites (including mange) can also cause bare crusty skin, which often appears between the toes, and if untreated spreads up the legs. Other parts of the body can also be susceptible to mite infestations. The mites are very small, and are difficult to see with the naked eye. To correctly diagnose this condition your vet will take a skin scraping and inspect it under the microscope where any mites will become visible. Treatment may include repeated injections of *ivermectin*.

Sunburn is not common in alpacas but can occur on white noses of young crias, especially suri. The nose can become quite blistered if not protected. Zinc ointment or long acting sunblock will give protection for a day or so. The skin soon darkens on most alpacas so sunburn is only a temporary problem. When you need to apply zinc or sunblock you will obviously have to catch the cria and hold it, which it may find quite stressful. After you have applied the ointment the cria will probably run to mum for comfort and a feed, so make sure the ointment has dried before letting the cria go or it may rub off on mum's udder.

PEM (polioencephalomalacia)

PEM is a rare but serious condition that most breeders will never experience, but it must be treated quickly if detected.

It is caused by thiamine deficiency, and is treated by replenishing the thiamine in the body with vitamin B1 injections.

Under normal conditions alpacas are able to make all the thiamine they need themselves, but if the rumen becomes unbalanced for any reason this process can suddenly stop and a thiamine deficiency results.

A sudden change in diet, stress, coccidia and lactic acidosis from too much grain are amongst the possible causes of PEM.

When introducing a new feed, do so slowly, so the rumen has time to adjust.

Symptoms of PEM

Thiamine is required for the brain to function normally and remain healthy. If there is a thiamine deficiency the brain swells and stops functioning in a normal manner. Symptoms therefore can include some very unusual behaviour triggered by the mal-functioning brain.

Some symptoms of PEM can also be typical of other ailments. These symptoms include listlessness, lethargy, lack of appetite, failure to keep up with the herd, and an unsteady gait or staggering. If you notice any of those symptoms it might be PEM - but probably it won't be. The following symptoms though are quite unusual and more likely to point to PEM:

- *"Stargazing" – head pointing upwards*
- *Apparent disorientation/blindness*
- *Walking in circles*
- *Running into fences, hyperactivity*

Treatment of PEM

If you suspect PEM ring your vet straight away. Your vet will probably give an immediate vitamin B1 injection (thiamine) possibly into the vein. If the condition is not PEM the B1 will do no harm (you cannot overdose vitamin B, the body excretes what it does not need), but if it is PEM it could be a life saver.

Grain overload

Alpacas love grain based pellets, and will also cheerfully scoff down the unprocessed grain itself if they have access to it. Too much grain, whether in pellet form or otherwise, is bad for them and can

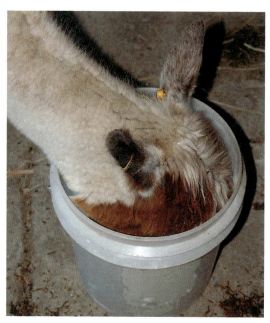

also cause PEM. It is compounded if they are not used to any grain in the diet. Grain overload can kill. Never give alpacas unrestricted access to grain.

Facial Eczema

Facial eczema (FE) can be a concern during the late summer and autumn, especially in the humid, warm northern regions of New Zealand. It also occurs in parts of Australia and has been recorded in other places in the world (South Africa and Oregon, USA).

Whilst it sounds rather like a complaint that a teenager might have when he looks in the mirror and *sees* pimples or spots on his face, it is in fact a completely unrelated condition and can be fatal. *Facial eczema* gets its name from the symptoms that affected animals can display, which include puffy eyes and peeling skin on the face and ears. But these symptoms are really a secondary result of liver damage, and it is the liver damage that is the real problem. The liver damage is caused by the spores of a fungus (*pithomyces chartarum*) that lives in the grass. This fungus is especially prevalent in rye grass. It thrives in the dead and decaying material at the base of the pasture, so grasses like kikuyu that form an elevated mat above the ground are less likely to harbour the fungus.

If you are in an area prone to FE you can check whether you have an unsafe level of spores in your own pasture by asking your vet to count them. You will need to provide the vet with a bag full of grass (a plastic "bread bag" full is the usual requirement), freshly cut from the paddock.

The grass must be dry, because the spore count will give you the ratio of spores to a kilo of pasture, and wet grass weighs more than dry grass. The grass should be carefully cut at the base of the leaves and stems, and as you handle the grass you must be careful not to wipe any potential spores away with your fingers or with the blades of the scissors. A small clump of grass should be cut from many places in the paddock, to give an even distribution of samples across the whole area being grazed. The vet will "wash" the grass in the correct volume of water and then, using a microscope, count the spores present in a drop of that water.

Alpacas are particularly susceptible to FE and a "low" spore count that is considered safe for other species may be too high for alpacas.

Avoiding FE

To combat FE you can feed zinc, or spray the paddocks to kill the fungus. Neither option is a perfect solution, but both help. Feeding zinc is often easiest.

A zinc block can be put in each water trough, this will help to provide some zinc to all the animals drinking from that trough, but it will not provide enough to fully protect the animals. Feeding *alpaca pellets* that have added zinc is a good solution if you have just a few alpacas and if they all enjoy the pellets (most do!), but it's not a solution if you have an animal that won't eat pellets, or you have bossy animals that scoff the lot so the shy ones miss out. In these cases individuals can be drenched with zinc - ask your vet for the correct volume and frequency.

Spraying paddocks to kill the fungus is a good option if you have paddocks that are easy to spray, but if they are steep and you need to engage a helicopter to do the job the cost may be prohibitive. Paddocks may need to be sprayed several times throughout the FE season as the fungus will return once the effect of the spray wears off. If you opt to spray the paddocks it is a good idea to conduct regular spore counts to be sure that the spray is still effective. Ask your vet or your local rural supply store for an appropriate spray.

Symptoms of FE

Symptoms of FE usually start with the animal seeking shade. This is because liver damage caused by the spores prevents the body from detoxifying and excreting the *chlorophyll* (green pigment) in the pasture, and the accumulation of this in the skin makes the animal sensitive to sunlight. This is known as *photosensitization*. The pink skin around the eyes can become very puffy

- if you see this during the FE season you should act immediately to prevent the disease from progressing further. As the disease progresses the skin on the face and other parts of the body may peel, and the tips of the ears may actually drop off.

Treatment of FE

Whilst damage to the liver is permanent, the liver is an organ that has an amazing capacity to re-grow, and affected animals can recover well if caught in time. Treatment involves moving the animal from the pasture into a dark environment – the less light the better, so a shed or barn is ideal. If the shed or barn is very open you may need to rig up screens or curtains of some sort to block the light.

Avoiding green feed helps to reduce the chlorophyll levels in the body, which will also aid in reducing the photosensitization. Once the photosensitization has reduced the animal will feel more comfortable, and it is now a matter of waiting for the liver to recover, so a long stay in the shed may be required. Of course, if an alpaca is confined to the shed you must ensure that it has company.

Your vet can take blood samples, and laboratory tests will indicate the level of liver damage. This will initially confirm the presence of FE in the body and later give an indication of the rate of recovery.

Broken bones

Keep an eye out for holes, especially rabbit holes, in your paddocks. A rabbit hole is just the right size to trap an alpaca's leg. If an unsuspecting alpaca running across the paddock puts its foot into a rabbit hole this can easily result in a broken bone. Symptoms will be obvious, and the vet's bill will follow!

Broken bones can also occur if a dam steps on her cria, especially if she steps on the cria's leg while it is in the kush position.

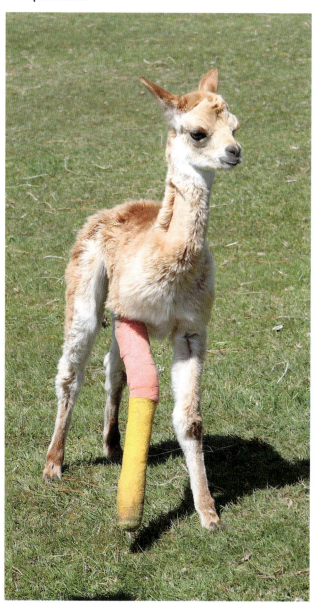

TB and Johne's Disease

Both TB (*tuberculosis*) and Johne's disease (*paratuberculosis*) have been reported in livestock in New Zealand, but very few (if any) of these reports involve alpacas. There is no requirement for alpaca owners to have their herds tested for these diseases. Alpacas being shown at A&P shows in New Zealand must belong to a herd that has a current "TB certificate" stating that the herd has been tested clear of TB, but if animals are not being shown there is no requirement for TB tests.

In the United Kingdom TB has been reported in alpacas and some herds have suffered several losses.

Identifying either of these two diseases is difficult as symptoms develop slowly, often over a period of years. Chronic weight loss, diarrhoea and breathing difficulties may be amongst the most obvious symptoms once the disease has progressed.

Poisoning

As discussed in the chapter on the farm environment, some trees are extremely poisonous, and some pasture weeds are also poisonous, but usually to a lesser extent. Generally, if an alpaca eats a small amount of poisonous pasture weed, the worst that will happen is that the alpaca will suffer from tummy ache.

Grazing animals will usually avoid poisonous plants, but if pasture is sparse they may be forced to eat plants that they would normally avoid. When poisonous plants are sprayed with weed killer they wilt and die and may become more palatable to grazing animals, so if you spray weeds make sure the alpacas do not have access to any that might contain toxins.

Moulds in feed can also cause toxins which may result in poisoning. If the feed looks or smells mouldy – don't use it!

Like horses, alpacas are susceptible to **ionophore poisoning**. *Ionophores* are additives included in poultry or cattle feed, often to protect against coccidia or to increase the efficiency of the feed and the speed at which a calf gains weight. Not all cattle feed contains ionophores, and if it does the packaging will mention it in the list of ingredients. Common ionophores in cattle feed are *Rumensin* and *Bovatec*.

No feed mill would deliberately include ionophores in dedicated alpaca feed, but if the mill does not have suitable precautions in place cross contamination can occur from one feed run to the next, and ionophores could accidentally slip in to the alpaca feed.

There was a well documented case of this in 2003 in Ohio, where the ionophore *salinomycin* contaminated a batch of alpaca feed, which resulted in hundreds of alpacas dying and hundreds more suffering damaged kidneys and hearts.

Now that feed mills are aware of the consequences of ionophore contamination for alpacas they may include a warning on certain bags of stock feed that the product is not to be fed to horses, llamas or alpacas. Whilst the feed itself does not have ionophores deliberately added, the manufacturer knows that there may be a risk of cross contamination, and so the warning on the bag should be taken seriously.

Infections and abnormal temperature

Most infectious diseases, skin abscesses or eye infections that are contracted by alpacas will respond to antibiotics either injected or applied topically. Your vet will advise and prescribe a suitable remedy.

Diagnosis of an infectious disease will include taking the alpaca's temperature.

The "normal" temperature range for alpacas is between 37.5°C and 39°C. This is quite a big range and so if an alpaca's temperature falls within it, it can be difficult to know whether that particular alpaca has an abnormally high or low temperature.

On a hot day, an unshorn alpaca may have a temperature just over 39°C. On a cold morning a temperature between 37°C and 37.5°C might be recorded. Generally, anything over 39°C or below 37°C is cause for concern. If you are worried about an animal and you take its temperature, and you get a result that is at the higher or lower end of the range and so is considered "normal", it might be a good idea to also take the temperatures of other alpacas (of a similar age and fleece length) as a comparison. If your subject alpaca has a temperature of 37.2°C and the others have temperatures ranging from 38.4°C to 38.7°C, then you should probably consider your subject to have a low temperature.

Infections can cause the temperature to either rise or fall outside the normal range. In some cases the temperature will fluctuate, so check it again in an hour or so.

The temperature is usually taken using a rectal thermometer. Make sure the bulb of the thermometer has contact with the body and is not reading the temperature of a clump of faeces!

Finally, if you notice **an alpaca sitting by itself away from the herd**, investigate. Alpacas like to stick together, they know there is safety in numbers. They are stoic creatures and often do not show any signs of illness until they can't hide it any longer. If an alpaca is too weak to keep up with the herd it needs your help. Check the body condition, check for anaemia by looking at the inner eye lid, take the temperature using a rectal thermometer, look for obvious signs of injury – and call the vet.

Some useful equipment:

- Nail clippers
- Zinc ointment
- Iodine
- Anti fungal ointment
- Oral drench syringe
- Rectal thermometer
- Sharp scissors - for trimming hair

Support groups

In most areas there will be other alpaca owners, and amongst these you will have a local support group to give advice and help if required. Most owners care deeply about their animals, and about alpacas in general, and so will offer the best advice that they can if you have a problem. Keep the phone numbers of local owners and breeders on hand, you can then talk through any issues with them. They may also have regular get-togethers, sometimes addressing specific topics, and this will be a good opportunity for you to gain knowledge and listen to other peoples' experiences.

SHEARING

Alpacas are usually shorn once a year, in the late spring or early summer. Shearing alpacas is an acquired skill and many sheep shearers will not tackle it. A fast, experienced shearer can shear an alpaca in just a few minutes and leave the animal looking very neat and tidy.

You can learn to shear them yourself, but most owners employ someone to do it for them. Specialist alpaca shearers tour the country, and if you contact them they will be able to advise when they will be in your area. Ask your local support group who you might contact in this regard.

Some shearers use a table to shear the alpacas, this makes the job easier and is less strain on the shearer's back. Whether shorn on the floor, or on a table, the alpaca will probably be restrained so that it does not kick or jump up and injure itself, or the shearer.

Most shearers use electric shearing equipment so a power supply is required. An extension lead will probably be needed, so make sure you have a suitable weatherproof extension lead that will be safe if it gets wet.

When the fleece is shorn off the animal, you will need to collect it. The blanket (i.e., the fleece from the main part of the body) is the most useful part of the fleece, so don't mix this up with the hairy brisket (chest) fleece, the belly

fleece, or the legs. Neck fleece is usually similar to the blanket in its style, but the staple length is often shorter.

If you want to have the fleece tested to measure its fineness tell the shearer and he will make sure you get a "mid side sample". The sample taken from the *mid side* point is reckoned to be indicative of the quality of the overall fleece, so taking a mid side sample is the most common method owners use to evaluate each fleece.

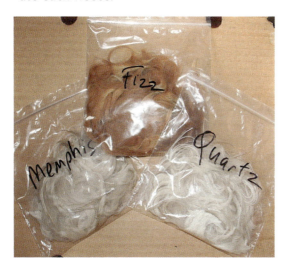

The easiest way to collect the mid side samples is to use small plastic sandwich bags, and write the alpaca's name on the outside with felt pen. Before shearing, ask your fleece testing lab what size fleece sample they require, as this can vary from lab to lab.

Shearers have their preferred shearing styles in both their shearing technique and the style of the "haircut" they give the alpaca. Some shearers take all the fleece off, from the toes to the top of the head. Most however will leave some hair on the head, sculpting it at the back into the shorn neck.

Most will leave a little hair just on the lower legs, some will sculpt the upper legs and leave some hair there too. If you have a preferred style of "haircut", tell the shearer before he starts.

Many owners take the opportunity of trimming toenails and giving injections while the animal is restrained. Some shearers have the equipment to trim teeth as well and will do this if required.

Later in the year, as the fleece grows, you may need to trim the hair on the head again so that it does not interfere with the alpaca's vision.

Understanding fleece test results

When you send a fleece sample to a wool testing lab they will analyse the fibres under magnification to measure the diameter of each fibre. The fibres are measured in microns. (A micron is one millionth of a metre, or a thousandth of a millimetre, so a micron measures 0.001mm.) The lab will then calculate the average diameter of all fibres in the sample, giving you the *micron average*.

Whilst the micron average is useful, it does not tell you the whole story. You need to know what the range of measurements were within the sample, and the report will also tell you this. Some of the fibres may be very fine, but some may be very coarse.

Alpaca fleece, like sheep's wool, is used predominately for clothing, and so an important question is "how prickly would clothing made from this fleece feel against the skin?". If fibre is over 30 microns in diameter it would feel prickly to most people, so you need to know how many fibres there were in the sample that were in excess of 30 microns.

Different fleece testing labs use different methods and equipment to measure the fibres. One of the most recently developed pieces of equipment is the OFDA 2000 (OFDA = Optical Fibre Diameter Analyser), which not only measures the diameter, but also the length of each fibre. It can therefore measure the diameter along the whole length of the fibre, showing variations in growth throughout the year.

The results of the test will be reported back to you by way of graphs showing *bell curves* giving the range of measurements of the fibres, and lists of figures that analyse the results, telling you how much variation there was between fibres in the sample.

Here are some commonly used terms that you may see in results:

SD - standard deviation
CV - co-efficient of variation
CF - comfort factor
PF - prickle factor
SF - spinning fineness
CRV - curve

The lower the SD, the less variation (*deviation*) there is in fibre diameter within the sample. The SD is measured in microns. The very best fleeces have SDs below 4 microns.

The CV is a mathematical calculation where the SD is expressed as a % of the average micron of the sample. Again, the lower the figure the better.

CF and PF give essentially the same information, but the first one tells you the percentage of fibres under 30 microns, and the second the percentage over 30 microns. It is sometimes expressed as % <30 or %>30. Either way, it tells you the same thing. A high CF is desirable, the best alpacas coming close to, or even equalling, 100%.

SF is another calculation, this time using the micron and the CV to give the estimated spinning fineness of the fleece.

CRV is expressed in degrees per mm and measures crimp in the fleece.

The graph is known as a histogram.

This is an example of a histogram from an alpaca with a fairly good fleece (note that CRV is low because the animal is suri):

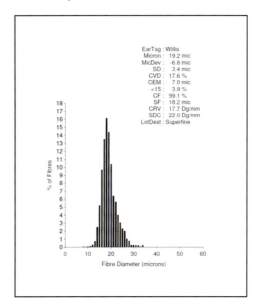

Below is a histogram from an alpaca with a poor fleece—note the wide base of the bell curve:

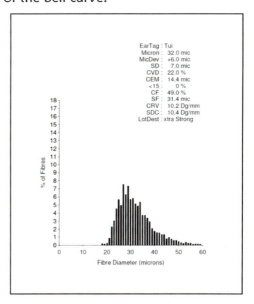

Fleece test results and Histograms from AAFT (Australian Alpaca Fibre Testing)

BREEDING

Breeding age

Ask 10 breeders at what age you should mate your females, and you will probably get 10 different answers. Some breeders say "when they are one year old", others wait until they are eighteen months old, and yet others will not mate their females until they are two or even three years old.

Some people go by weight, and mate them once they have reached 45 Kg. Others use the dam's weight as a base and mate the daughter when she has reached 80% of that weight.

I tend to take a combined approach—if she is at least a year old, and big enough, and keen to mate, then she can.

Some females show willing at quite a young age, sitting while another mating is taking place when they are six months old or less. Others don't want to mate even when they are two years old. These are extremes though, and the average alpaca female will mate quite readily at a year or so of age,

Males tend to mature later, many not being interested until they are over two years of age, and some not "performing" until they are three.

However, they may be capable (and keen) from a year of age or less, so be aware of this if you have big male crias in the paddock, and keep an eye on their behaviour. If a cria is precocious, move him out of the paddock when he is six months old—even if he is not capable yet of actually mating a female, he will certainly be annoying them by jumping on them.

Gestation

Alpacas are usually pregnant for over 11 months. The "average" gestation period is reckoned to be 342 days. Research done by various people, in various parts of the world, give averages between 336 and 350 days. A perfectly normal cria can be born after just 10 months (around 305 days) gestation, but usually such a short gestation would result in a premature cria. It is unusual for gestation to last over 12 months, but it does happen.

Prepare for a cria from 10 months onwards, expect it after 11 months, but don't be surprised if you have to wait almost a year.

Naomi, at 9 months of age—ready, willing, but not old enough to mate. A female alpaca, keen for sex, can be quite difficult to move!

Anatomy

As with all mammals, female alpacas have two *ovaries*. They are tiny, measuring approximately 1.1cm by 1.6cm. The ovaries are connected to the uterus via *uterine tubes*, which in turn connect to the *uterine horns*. The uterus has two horns, the right horn and the left horn. Pregnancies usually occur in the left horn, regardless of which ovary produced the egg to be fertilised. When you look at a heavily pregnant alpaca you can often see that the cria is positioned on the left side – i.e., the bulge is bigger on that side.

Mating

Most breeders "pen" mate their alpacas. This means that they know the date that the mating took place, they know for certain which male was used, they were able to observe the female's response to the male, and they could oversee the mating to know whether the male "got it right".

Females are ready to mate again two or three weeks after giving birth. This effectively means that there will be an annual turnaround, and the next cria will be born at the same time of year -

essential in the harsh mountainous climate where the alpaca evolved.

Like cats, female alpacas are induced ovulators. They are receptive at any time when not pregnant, and the act of mating causes them to ovulate. Most alpacas will ovulate within a few days after mating. If the female is re-introduced to the male before she ovulates she will still be receptive, but if she is re-introduced after she ovulates she will not be.

A typical mating may last for half an hour or more. The male approaches the female, *orgling* loudly. The sound of the orgling, combined with the male's confident approach, causes the female to sit and allow him to mate her. Males are trickle ejaculators, and ejaculate frequently throughout the event. They re-position the penis regularly, from one horn of the uterus to the other, ejaculating into each horn. This is so that there will be semen in both horns, which can travel into both uterine tubes. It doesn't matter which ovary produces the egg, there will be semen there to fertilise it.

Ovulation causes the infertile egg to be released from the ovary. By now the semen has travelled sufficiently far into each uterine tube to allow fertilisation of the newly released egg to take place, no matter which ovary has produced the egg.

The fertilised egg moves freely within the uterus for a few weeks, and then attaches itself to the wall of the uterine horn (usually the left horn) where it starts to develop a placenta. It will stay there and grow for the rest of the gestation period.

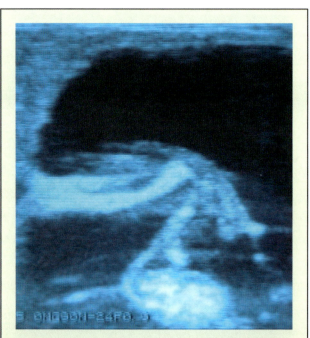

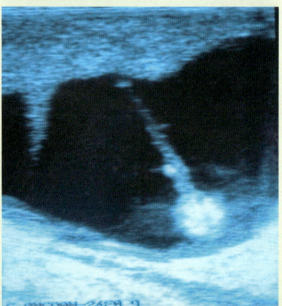

Pregnancy can be confirmed by ultrasound scans. The foetus is often visible after 42 days gestation. The dark area is the fluid filled uterus, the developing foetus is usually seen initially as a white "blob" attached to the uterine wall by an umbilical cord. As the foetus develops bones can be seen. However scans do not always detect a pregnancy, especially late in the term.

Different females behave differently when mated. In a "text book" mating the male will approach the female, orgle seductively, and she will sit almost immediately and allow the mating to take place. However, some males are sexier than others! Females generally prefer a confident approach, and they will sit more readily for a confident male than they will for a nervous one.

Some females are desperate to get pregnant and will sit for any male, no matter how young or inexperienced. Others require a lot more persuasion.

Nervous females may sit out of fear, or equally, refuse to mate out of fear. These females can be very difficult to read when conducting matings or *spit offs*.

When a mating is taking place other empty females are likely to come and sit beside the mating couple, effectively saying "me next!". This is sometimes a good solution to the problem of shy maidens, as they can become aroused by the activity and choose to sit in their own time without feeling threatened and overwhelmed by the male's approaches.

Young male crias will often also be excited by the spectacle of the mating, and will join in, climbing on top of the mating couple or on to any waiting females.

Spit offs

After a female has mated and has *ovulated*, she will refuse to mate again. To test that ovulation really has occurred many breeders will conduct a *spit off* a week after mating. The female is re-introduced to the male, and if she has ovulated she will refuse his advances. Her normal reaction is to spit at him – hence the term "spit off". Some females don't spit, but run and try to escape; this is still an obvious rejection of the male's advances.

However, ovulation does not guarantee that conception will take place. If conception does take place, it will do so within two weeks of mating. A spit off is therefore usually conducted around 14 days after mating, and if the female spits at that point it is considered that she is pregnant. If she is receptive to the male we know that conception did not take place, and she can mate again.

Pregnancies can occasionally fail for some reason after conception has taken place, and many breeders conduct several spit offs, especially early in the term, to be sure that the pregnancy is holding.

Another way to confirm pregnancy is by an ultrasound scan—this can be useful in the case of nervous females who are difficult to read during a spit off.

Unpacking

Alpaca breeders use the term "unpacking" to refer to the act of birthing. It is obviously a play on words and it describes the event very well. Most of the time births take place uneventfully, and the first that the owner knows of the birth is that there is a new cria trotting happily along behind its mother in the paddock.

Whilst the majority of births take place in the morning or very early afternoon, occasionally births take place in the evening or at night. A late birth may indicate a problem, but this is not necessarily so.

Signs that the female is about to unpack are often easily missed, and in some cases the signs are pretty much non-existent. Sometimes it is clear – the dam moves purposefully away from the herd, sniffing the ground and looking for a clean place to have the cria, or she sits down and rolls vigorously on her side. Her behaviour may change for the few days leading up to the birth, she may hold back at feeding time when she would normally be the first in line, and she may have developed quite a large udder. From these last two signs you will know that she will have the baby soon, but you won't know when. All you can do is keep an eye on her and watch for any signals that she has gone into labour or is about to unpack. But some females do not allow the mere fact that they are having a baby interfere with their lifestyle at all, and these females give no obvious warning of the impending birth.

With a normal birth either the nose or the front feet can be presented first. More often than not the head comes out first, followed by the two front feet, but in some cases the feet and legs appear before the head. Either way, the emergence of the head, the right way up, and both front legs indicates that the cria is correctly positioned for birthing. Once the skull has fully appeared the neck can slip through the birth canal quite quickly, and it is only the shoulders that may create a sticking point. The shoulders are the widest part of the body, once they have emerged the rest of the birth is quite quick.

Most females birth standing up, but to help the process along many will intermittently sit down in the kush position and then lie on their sides to roll vigorously.

Ideally the cria should hang out of the dam for long enough to allow the lungs to clear of any fluids. When the cria falls to the ground it lands in an ungainly heap and wriggles to right itself. This wriggling removes the protective membrane. Alpaca mothers do not eat the membrane or clean the cria up, the cria effectively cleans itself up. The cria should be in the kush position within a few minutes.

The next step for the cria is to struggle to its feet, and the next step for the dam is to expel the placenta. Once the cria is up on its feet it will look for the udder. Often the cria will be looking for the udder, and may even be feeding, before the placenta is passed.

The placenta usually appears as a big bluish tinged sac filled with liquid. It slowly emerges and inches downwards,

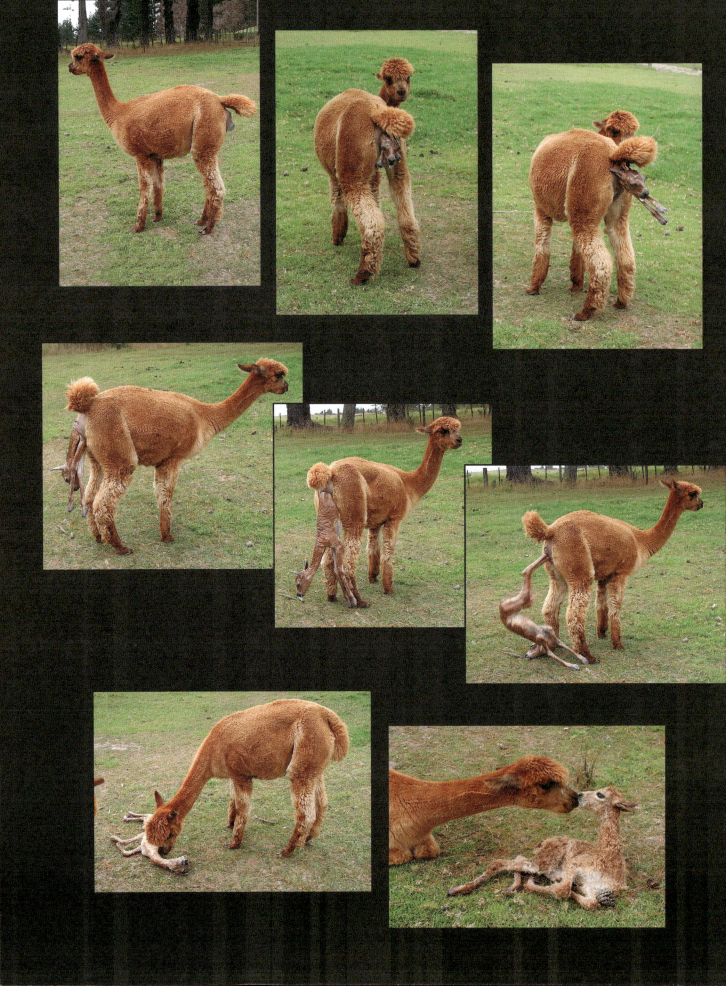

finally falling to the ground with the rest of the placenta following behind.

It is vitally important that the cria feeds within 12 to 24 hours as it needs colostrum while it can still process this. Colostrum contains the necessary antibodies to protect the cria from infections for the first few weeks of its life. Most crias will be feeding long before 12 hours is up though, with the majority managing this within an hour or two.

When the placenta has passed it is a good idea to check that it is all there and that no part of it has been retained in the uterus. A retained placenta can cause infection as it starts to decompose inside the body. If you spread it out on the ground you should see both horns.

If part – or all – of it has been retained call the vet.

Problem births

Whilst the vast majority of births are perfectly normal, occasionally things can go wrong. If there is a problem during birth this is known as a *dystocia*.

Most dystocias will actually be fairly minor and easy to resolve, and once the problem is corrected the birth will be normal. Sometimes the cria just gets stuck – often at the shoulders – and a gentle tug from the owner will help to move things along. Remember if you do need to help that the natural path is out and down, not straight out horizontally, so guide the cria downwards as you pull. If the dam needs help she will probably let you know and will welcome your "interference" by pushing as you pull. If you come across her during the birthing process and you have no idea when she started, and she looks exhausted or appears to have given up, your help will probably be welcome. But if the dam is doing alright by herself, don't interfere!

If once the head and legs have appeared you notice that one leg looks longer than the other, then the shorter leg is probably folded at the elbow and may be caught on the dam's pelvic bone. Just pulling gently on the leg could release it - if not you may need to push the cria back a little to give more room to straighten the leg.

Breech births can often resolve themselves without assistance as long as the back legs are correctly extended. However if the birth does not progress quickly the cria can suffocate before the head emerges, so if you are there you can speed things up a little, increasing the cria's chances of survival.

Other dystocias are more serious, including breech birth without the back legs extended, and other unusual presentations by the cria. Such presentations could include a cria with one leg back, or its head back, or the cria in an upside down position. If you think you have a serious problem call the vet immediately.

And, as a general rule, if the female is clearly distressed and has been in labour for some hours, call the vet.

On rare occasions you may see a *prolapse*: the uterus has been expelled with the cria, and hangs outside the body. Don't confuse the prolapsed uterus with the placenta. The placenta sac has a shiny smooth surface and is filled with dark, bluish liquid whereas the uterus looks meaty and flesh like. The vet can replace the uterus into the body, and should be called as quickly as possible to attend to this.

While you wait, keep the uterus as clean and moist as you can, placing the female on a tarpaulin or mat of some sort, and putting a cool damp towel over the uterus.

Tui's story:

Tui prolapsed with her first cria. I came home from work to find her sitting with her uterus on the ground; I called the vet who duly replaced it and she was fine. I didn't re-mate her for about a year, to give her time to fully recover.

With the second pregnancy she started to bulge alarmingly at the rear end, and for the few weeks before she unpacked her uterus protruded regularly (top photo).

I was convinced she would prolapse again with this second cria, so I checked on her frequently as she got closer to her "due" date, usually with my cell phone in hand with the vet's number displayed ready to dial. At 12.30 on the day the cria was born she showed no signs whatsoever of unpacking, she was happily sitting amongst the other females in the shade of a big pine tree. When I went back into the paddock an hour and a half later there was the cria on the ground, struggling to stand. Tui's uterus thankfully was still inside her body.

I watched her pass the placenta, and she did it very, very carefully. She started off sitting down, with her rear end pointing up hill, as the placenta slowly inched out (bottom photo). Perhaps she deliberately sat this way so that gravity would help to keep the uterus in place?

Eventually she stood, and in a very controlled way she let the placenta creep towards the ground, not letting it go until she was sure it was safe to do so.

I wondered whether she had unpacked the same way, and, by being careful, had avoided a second prolapse. Perhaps she learnt from her mistakes the first time!

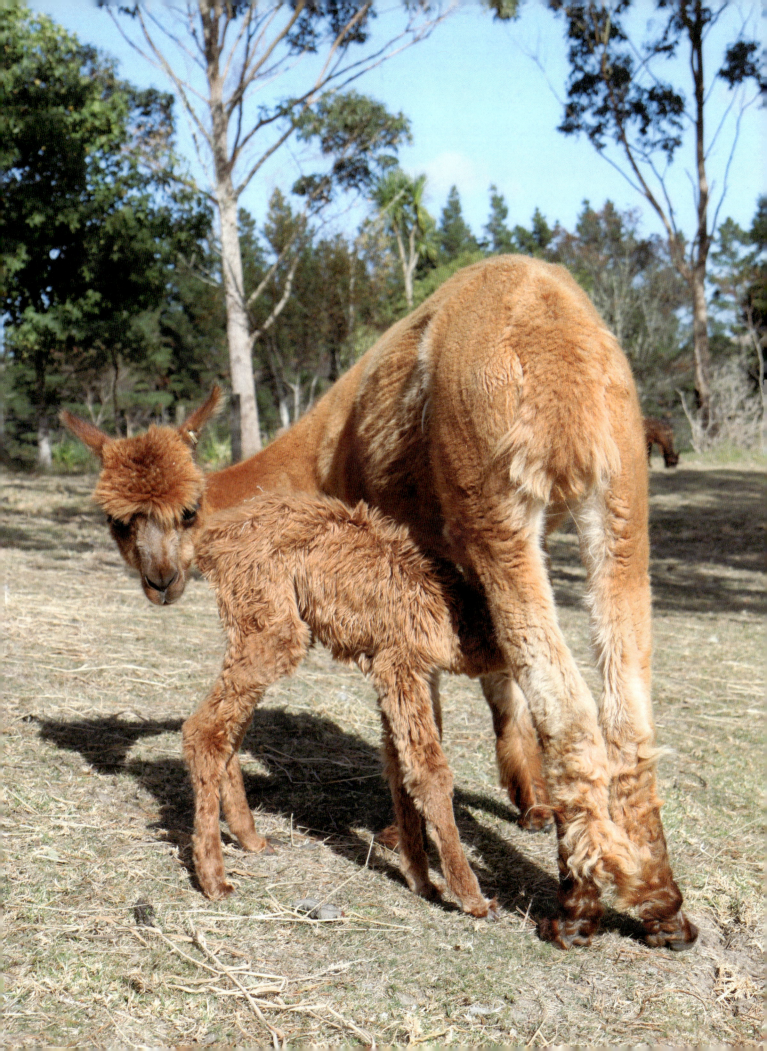

CRIAS

The newborn cria

Once the cria is born you should check that it is fit and well and then leave it to bond with its mother. Check that the airways are not blocked by the protective membrane, that the cria has all its necessary body parts and is not deformed in any way, and that the umbilical cord is not bleeding.

Many breeders will spray iodine on the umbilical cord at this point to ensure that the cria does not suffer from "navel ill", or infections transmitted through a poorly sealed umbilical cord.

If you think the cria looks small or weak, weigh it. You can then weigh it again each day until you are satisfied that it is gaining weight and growing.

Expect a newborn cria to weigh somewhere between 5kg and 10kg.

Regularly check on the cria until you see it suckling. If you stand close enough you should hear the slurping sounds – then you know it really is feeding. The cria's first attempts to suckle can be quite frustrating for the human observer, it looks in the wrong places, and when finally it finds the right place its head pops out from underneath the dam having gone right under the belly. Then at last it finds the udder but doesn't manage to latch on to a teat. Eventually though it does find a teat, and all should now be well.

Crias "snack" – they feed often, every couple of hours, and for just a few minutes at a time. If you notice that a cria is attempting to feed more frequently than once an hour or so, then it is probably hungry and the dam may not have enough milk. Check the udder, and if it seems to be constantly empty you will need to supplement the cria's milk supply.

If for any unlikely reason the dam cannot (or does not) feed the cria at all, you may be the sole provider of milk.

Bottle feeding

Baby bottles designed for human babies work quite well for crias, as do plastic bottles with lamb teats. For the first 24 hours feed only colostrum. You can buy frozen colostrum or powdered colostrum, but either way it cannot be heated in the microwave or the antibodies will be destroyed. Ask you vet's advice as to the best colostrum to use.

Once the 24 hours is up you can start to introduce milk into the feed. Milk powder designed for lambs is usually used for crias, but again, be advised by your vet. Aim to feed the equivalent of 10% of the cria's body weight each day, spread over four to six feeds.

When you bottle feed a cria, try to make the cria stand in the same position as it would normally stand when nursing on the udder. This ensures that the neck is held at the correct angle so the feed will find its way to the stomach and not end up in the lungs.

As the cria grows and matures you can reduce the number of feeds per day.

If the cria is too weak to suckle, call the vet. He or she can then *tube feed* the cria – that is, feed the cria through a thin plastic tube that has been slid down the neck into the stomach.

Be careful when bottle feeding that the cria does not become too friendly, especially if the cria is male. It is very tempting when he is a cute little baby to want to cuddle him and to let him smooch around you. When he grows up he will not be so cute, and if he is confused as to whether he is alpaca or human – or whether you are alpaca or human – he may try to dominate you. You do not want to be dominated by a 100kg male alpaca – so feed the cria without any fuss, then send him back to his herd. The same is true with any overly friendly cria, whether you are bottle feeding or not. Make sure that you do not encourage them to play with you when they are little, and then to play fight when they get bigger, and finally to challenge your leadership when they grow up.

Cria coats

If a cria is premature (not full term) or dysmature (full term but not fully mature) it may have difficulty in regulating its body temperature. This is especially dangerous if the cria is born into poor weather conditions. For a few days you should make sure that it keeps warm. If it is not warm enough you will need to help by keeping it warm until it is mature enough to regulate its own temperature. You can either put mum and baby into a dry, draught free shed, or you can put a coat on baby. In some cases you might even do both.

Even full term, fully mature newborn crias can benefit from a coat if the weather is particularly cold or wet. Suri crias are affected by wet conditions more than huacaya crias because the fleece soaks through more easily.

If you are using a cria coat make sure that the dam will accept her baby when it is covered. If the mother doesn't recognise her baby she may reject it, or worse, attack it. Most dams don't mind the coat at all, but if you are using one and you don't know her likely reaction, proceed with caution. Alpacas recognise their crias partly by their appearance and partly by their scent. A cria coat should not cover the cria's tail, because this is one of the main places that the dam will sniff her cria. It is better for a coat to be too short than too long.

To lessen the chance of the dam rejecting the cria in a coat you could try rubbing the outside of the coat onto the cria's fleece (transferring the cria's scent onto the coat) or perhaps rubbing the coat onto the dam. If you can find a coat that is the same colour as the cria the cria's appearance will change less, and there is less risk of the dam not recognising the cria visually.

The first few days

When there's a new cria on the ground the rest of the herd will be curious and want to learn about it, coming over to

sniff it and to say hello. Some dams allow this, but others may be very protective for the first few days of the cria's life. A dam like this will keep the cria well away from the rest of the herd, and well away from the prying human. She may hold back at feeding time, not wanting to risk exposing her baby to the crowd. If the cria wanders off she will hum anxiously and call it back. Other dams however carry on exactly as normal, allowing their crias to socialise right from the start, and bringing them to the feed area on the very first day.

Weaning

Left to their own devices, most females wean their crias when the next pregnancy has advanced to around nine or ten months. If the dam is not pregnant she may allow the cria to feed for up to two years.

If the cria is female, and assuming that the stud male is not running with the mob of females, then it is probably a good solution to let the dam wean the cria herself. But if the cria is male and is making a nuisance of himself he should be weaned earlier, as long as he is over five or six months old. It is very unlikely that a male would be fertile at such a young age but if he is precocious it would be wise to move him away from the girls.

When the dam weans the cria herself the cria knows where it stands, and will soon learn that the milk bar has closed. If the human moves the cria away from the dam before she was ready to wean it, and then, because the cria is female, moves her back some months later, she will go straight back to mother who will quite possibly let her feed again.

However, if the dam is in poor health and at risk herself, it may be necessary to remove the cria as soon as it is self sufficient so that the demands on mum are kept to a minimum.

BREEDING FOR COLOUR

Alpacas come in a wide range of colours, ranging from white through fawns and browns to black. Black alpaca is true black, unlike the dull brown "black" that sheep breeders must contend with.

Alpaca black doesn't fade either, it stays black. Some alpacas may bleach a little at the tips of the fleece as the year progresses but many stay exactly the same colour as the day they were shorn.

Fawns can be very pale, almost white, but when the animal is wet, or the fleece is spun, the colour is more apparent. Fawns then move through the shades to brown. Dark brown is almost black; these are the alpacas you look at and say "is it brown—or is it black?".

There are two hues of brown—a yellowish brown, and a rich vibrant mahogany red.

More colours are created when the grey gene is present, with silver grey and many shades of rose grey being possible.

When black crias are born some appear brown. This is because the uterine fluids have bleached the fleece on the developing foetus. As the cria grows, and the fleece grows, the true colour will start to emerge. It is quite common to see an apparently brown cria with very black fleece at the skin. Once this cria has been shorn it will obviously be a black animal. The same is true with greys. Some appear rose grey when born but as the fleece grows it becomes obvious that they are actually silver grey.

Silver grey alpacas are really black alpacas with the grey effect created by a *white marking* gene.

This white marking gene can be over any colour base, so dark brown alpacas with the gene become dark rose grey, and light brown and fawn ones become lighter rose greys. Some lovely colours are possible when the grey gene is present. Grey alpacas usually have white faces, and often white legs and white bellies.

Because alpaca colours are so clean and vibrant, many breeders choose to breed for colour. When it comes to clothing, black is always in fashion! Fawn and grey are also ideal for clothing—and yes, of course there is a place for white. White can be blended with any other colour to lighten it or it can be used alone.

White is obviously the preference of commercial mills and clothing manufacturers because it can be dyed any colour. If you want to breed alpacas with the long term aim of selling the fleece for this use, then white is the best colour to breed. Aim for white alpacas with fleeces that do not have spots or guard hair in any other colour. Dark hairs in the fleece will show as dark flecks in the finished product.

If you want to use your fleeces yourself without dying them, and your fawn is a little darker than you would like, then blend it with white. Like mixing paint, a little colour goes a long way. If you mixed together three dark fawn fleeces and one white one you would hardly notice the lightening effect, but if you put one dark fawn fleece in with three white ones you should obtain a pleasing delicate fawn colour as a result. Try experimenting with a few staples from each fleece to get an idea of the volumes needed to achieve the colour you want.

So even if you choose to breed for colour your white fleeces will also be useful.

Breeding black alpacas is generally easy as long as you start with black dams and you always use black sires. There can be no guarantees that all the crias will be black, but you would expect black in the vast majority of cases.

Many brown alpacas are also carrying black, so mating a black to a brown may produce black, but it may also produce brown in any shade.

To breed white you would use white sires over white dams, and most of the crias would be white. However any other colour could also eventuate and you would expect a few fawns, along with the occasional brown, and very rarely, black.

Breeding for fawn can be difficult. A fawn breeder once told me that he'd

been breeding that colour for years and that he hardly ever got fawn crias—he got browns and whites, but the fawns were few and far between. This may be because fawn tends to occur quite frequently when a white is mated to a brown or black, so fawn alpacas are often carrying other colours.

The lightest fawns often fade as they grow up, and within a few months they look completely white. Darker fawns usually stay the same colour.

If you want to breed a grey cria, at least one of the parents must have this gene. If you have a solid coloured black female and you mate her to a grey sire you have a 50% chance of getting a grey cria and a 50% chance of getting a black one. However, if your female is tuxedo (white on the face, neck or feet) or piebald (irregular white patches anywhere on the body) the equation becomes much more complicated and you may end up with a white cria with blue eyes that is also deaf.

These white alpacas with blue eyes are known as *blue eyed whites*, or *BEWs* for short. A BEW comes about when an alpaca inherits two different white marking genes, one from each parent. Not all BEWs have fully blue eyes, and not all are deaf. The deafness is caused by a lack of *melanin* (black pigment) in the body, which is also the reason for the white fleece and the sky blue (actually, colourless) eyes.

Blue eyes are associated with greys and a BEW will always have one parent carrying the grey pattern. This grey pattern may be quite visible, as it is on a silver grey, but it might be difficult to see, as it is on a light fawn.

Sometimes the white marking on a tuxedo or piebald is very small and hardly noticeable. A tuxedo may have just one tiny white spot on the face or under the chin. However, the tuxedo gene is present, and so is the risk of a BEW cria if this alpaca is mated to a grey.

This does not mean that all BEWs will produce black or silver grey crias. If you own a BEW female with one black and one grey parent, and you always mate her to a solid coloured black sire, then you can expect black or grey crias.

But if she has only white and fawn in her ancestry it is unlikely that she will throw a black cria. Just because she has inherited these two different white patterns doesn't mean that she has inherited a dark colour base on which to display them.

Full brother and sister, one is a piebald huacaya and the other is a grey suri. They are progeny of the BEW female on the opposite page. Their sire is a solid black suri, heterozygous for the suri gene.

It is desirable in alpacas for the fleece to be even in colour throughout the blanket. A blotchy brown, for instance, with dark or light patches or spots, is not as desirable as a consistently coloured brown.

Greys however often have spots, and they are tolerated in a grey. It is unusual for a grey to be evenly coloured throughout the fleece.

Whilst it is not considered desirable for the fibre market, a few breeders deliberately breed *fancies*. Piebalds and appaloosas are considered "fancy". Fancies can be quite eye catching and a big hit with the public. If breeding for piebald or appaloosa, a pleasing pattern is the aim.

The *wild marking* is the pattern seen on vicuña and guanaco. The body is brown, or perhaps dark fawn, and under the belly is white or light fawn.

The alpaca on the opposite page is suri, with a solid black sire and a solid brown dam. The alpaca on this page is huacaya, with a solid black sire and a solid white dam. The two animals are not related. Whilst many fawn alpacas fade to a lighter colour under the belly both of these have dramatic markings with a clear division between the darker and lighter colours.

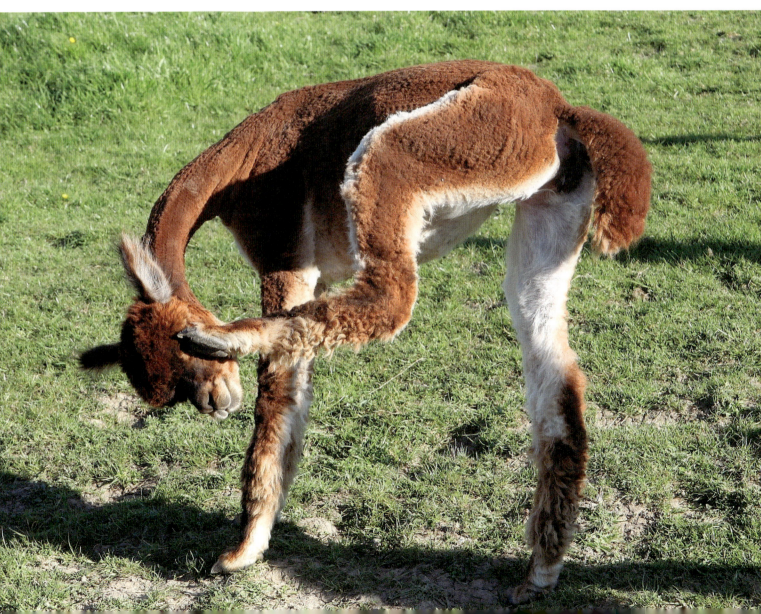

SHOWING ALPACAS

Many Agricultural and Pastoral Associations have local annual shows that include an alpaca section. You can learn a lot about alpacas, and what characteristics are desirable, if you watch one of these shows and listen to the judge's comments.

Judges usually look for fineness in the fleece, density, brightness or lustre, and evenness of crimp or lock style across the body. The fleece must also have a pleasing "handle" – that is, it feels nice to the touch. Judges also check the teeth and genitalia, and expect to see good conformation in the exhibits. They like to see breeding males with a strong, robust and masculine frame.

If you are a member of the Alpaca Association and your alpacas are registered with them, you can enter your alpacas in to a show. The animals must be halter trained, and in New Zealand must belong to a herd that has been tested as being clear of TB.

Showing your alpacas is a good way to meet other breeders, and by listening to the judge's comments, to make breeding decisions for your own animals.

PHOTOGRAPHING YOUR ALPACAS

Even with a modest compact camera anyone can take great photographs of their alpacas. The keys to a good photo are *lighting*, *composition* and *the angle of the shot*.

What you must remember is that you have a brain and the camera does not. When you look at a scene your brain interprets what you see, but when your camera is pointed at the scene it records exactly what is there. If you are looking into the light your brain compensates for this, and you see the subject quite clearly. Your camera on the other hand *sees* the bright light, and the photo it takes of the subject will be dark and under exposed.

As for composition, you may see a group of three alpacas at the bottom of your paddock, standing nicely and looking at you – so you take a photo. The camera sees the group of three alpacas, and the big truck passing by, and the blue plastic drum that you meant to move out of the paddock last week, and the telegraph pole growing out of the alpaca's head, and the fence with the broken post, and the house across the road that needs painting, and so on.

So to take good photos all you have to do is to learn to see what is actually there, not what your brain tells you is there. If the sun is behind you, or to the side, the lighting should be fine. If the sun is in front of you the photo will probably be a disappointment because you will be looking straight into the light. If there is no sun, and the day is bleak with poor natural light, the photo will be flat and uninteresting.

When considering the composition look critically at everything that is in the camera's field of vision; the background is as important as the subject and can detract from the photo. With digital cameras if the subject does not fill the frame you can crop the photo in the computer, but if the subject is very small it might be disappointingly fuzzy by the time you have removed the unnecessary space around it.

If you are using an auto focus camera make sure it focuses on the right thing, not on the spindly tree branch that you didn't notice that was close to you or the fence post in the distance. You don't have to hold the camera in a horizontal position—it will function just as well if you hold it vertically, and the composition might be more pleasing. In many cases with alpaca photos a vertical composition is much better, so analyse the shot before you take it.

Most people are used to viewing the world from their own eye level, but sometimes this is not the best angle for the photograph. Getting down lower, or climbing up higher, could completely change the picture. For a start, it will move the background – it might improve dramatically. But more importantly it will change the view of the subject. If you photograph a cria from a standing position you will be looking down on it, but if you squat down or hold the camera at a lower level you

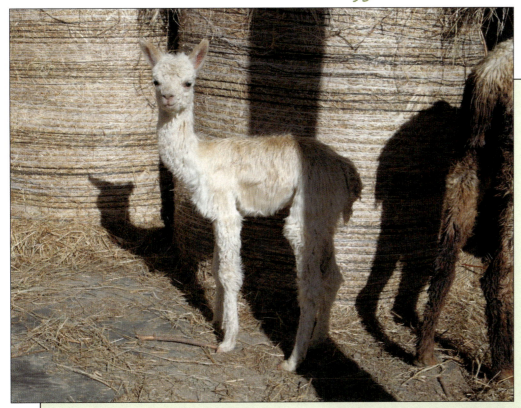

Here are two photos of the same cria, taken just a few minutes apart.

In the first photo there is a shadow falling on the back legs and rump of the cria, and there is an adjacent animal casting an annoying shadow on the hay bale to the right of the cria.

The first photo is also taken in landscape format.

In the second photo the cria has moved and the shadow has gone.

Also, the cria fills the frame because the shot is in portrait format rather than landscape.

The angle has also changed.

In the first photo the camera is looking down on the cria.

The second photo is taken from a lower point so the cria's face is at the same level as the lens.

Here are two more photos taken a few minutes apart, The first photo is taken against the light and so the sky looks overcast with the alpacas looking dull and under exposed. The second photo is taken from the other side of the mound of rock so the light has changed dramatically, and now the sky is blue and the alpacas are well lit.

will see it face to face.

This is especially important when photographing a stud male. Do you want him to look short and inferior or tall and imposing?

If you have a high megapixel camera, and you intend to send a photo of your animals to a friend by email, resize the photo before you send it. Firstly crop the photo so the subject fills the frame. If the file is still large, resize the photo so it can be comfortably viewed on the screen – don't leave it at a size where the recipient has to scroll from side to side and top to bottom to view it.

Besides, the larger the file the longer it will take to send, and the more space it takes up in the recipient's mail box.

And lastly, if you have a digital camera, take lots of photos. It's not as if you are using a conventional film camera with just 24 frames on the film and with expensive printing costs. If you take several shots of the same subject at least one of them should have perfect focus and composition, with just the right angle of the alpaca's head and ears. If they are all good there will probably be subtle differences between them. You can then choose the best one and delete all the others.

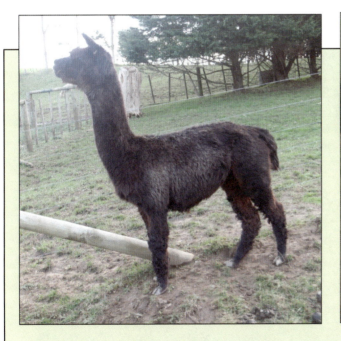

Black alpacas can be very difficult to photograph, with the black either washing out to become very pale and dull or darkening to the point that it becomes featureless. This happens when the camera doesn't know which part of the scene to read, and when the light is wrong. To get good photos of black animals make sure that you focus on the animal itself so that the camera reads the black rather than the surrounding area, and make sure that the light source is behind you or to the side. Never try to photograph a black animal when you are looking in to the light. In the photo on the right, the camera has focused on the lighter black of the fleece—i.e., where the fleece is reflecting back the light, so the darker areas appear very black, giving a good punchy shot.

VISITORS TO THE PADDOCK

Alpacas are ideal animals to interact with visitors to the paddock. They are gentle with babies, children and elderly people, but of course some basic rules must be observed.

Remind your visitors that alpacas are farm animals, not pets, and do not want to be patted or stroked or played with like the family dog. Having said that, if humans enter the paddock with buckets of feed the alpacas will probably mob them. If the visitors are elderly, frail, or very young, make sure they are not knocked over by enthusiastic alpacas keen to sample whatever is in the buckets.

When visitors come it's a good idea to have feed on hand that is safe if consumed in some volume, because the cheekiest and greediest alpacas are likely to get more than their fair share of what's on offer.

Lucerne based pellets (or similar) with little or no grain content are safest if you use commercially prepared feed. And willow branches make a good healthy treat that the alpacas will enjoy, with the advantage that several can eat from the same branch at once.

Warn your visitors that alpacas are naturally defensive animals and don't like surprise approaches, especially towards their rear ends. Explain to them that they should not do this because some alpacas may kick if they are surprised or feel threatened.

If the would-be visitors to the paddock cannot get there, selected alpacas can be taken to visit them. Well behaved halter trained alpacas make good PR animals and are ideal to take to rest homes, schools etc.

If you plan to take your alpaca to visit a rest home or school, make sure that he can cope with the various floor surfaces that he is likely to encounter. Practice walking him on carpet, tiles, polished wooden or terrazzo flooring and vinyl or linoleum covered floors. Practice taking him inside buildings so that he is not put off by the narrow doors and hallways. Also watch for any tell tale

signs that he needs a toilet break (like lifting his tail) and move him outside pronto if you think this might happen!

And finally, when your alpacas interact with visitors to your farm, or with people you visit, be sure to have your camera with you and take lots of photos.

When you view your photos later you'll be surprised at the interaction and eye contact between alpacas and people, and the looks of delight on the faces of your visitors.

Then send copies of the photos to the people concerned and delight them again!

USING THE FLEECE

Skirting the fleece

Before you can use the fleeces from your animals you need to go through each one and pull out all the debris, and also *skirt* the fleece.

Skirting involves spreading the whole fleece out and looking objectively at it, and then pulling out the bits that are clearly of lower quality. These will be the parts containing more of the stiff guard hair, or the parts that are generally coarser in micron than the main body of the fleece.

A *skirting table* is useful here, but you can spread the fleece out on anything. A skirting table is usually made from wire or plastic netting stretched over a wooden frame. When the fleece is spread out on this netting some of the debris will fall through the holes, making your job easier.

The poorer quality fleece will be found on the legs, under the belly, across the brisket (chest) and in the "armpits". Your shearer may have separated these out for you at the time of shearing, but often bits get missed. Put aside the poorer quality fleece, it may be useful for stuffing small soft toys or pet duvets or the like, or as garden mulch.

Once you have removed the poorer quality fleece you should sort through what's left on the table and pick out all the vegetation matter. Some fleeces are easy to clean with very little vegetation, others seem to have attracted every bit of hay, and every leaf fragment and

seed in the paddock, and have some kind of magnetic quality that holds it all there.

If you get the fleece professionally carded this process will remove some of the debris, but not all of it. Besides, the more debris that is in the fleece you send off, the greater the loss will be during carding. This is because the carding process will not only remove the larger pieces of debris but also the fleece that it caught around them.

Skirting is very important when you are showing fleeces at A & P shows. The judge will deduct points for poorly skirted fleeces, and for contamination by vegetation, or foreign colours in the blanket. Judges look for an even coloured fleece with consistent staple length and style. If your black alpaca has a white spot in the middle of the blanket, remove it when you skirt the fleece. If you were to card and then spin that fleece with the white spot still in place there would be white fibres all through the finished yarn.

Washing the fleece

Whether you intend to card the fleece yourself at home using hand carders or a small drum carder, or to get it carded professionally, it is a good idea to wash your fleece before it is carded. You can do this at home, or if you are getting it carded professionally, the carding company may be prepared to wash it for you. If the fleece is not washed it will produce a lot of dust as it goes through the carding rollers (and the person operating the carding machinery will not thank you for this) and the end result will be a dirty fleece for you to spin.

When you wash a fleece it should be handled gently or it will start to turn into felt. You must be careful not to felt it during the washing process by using water that is too hot, or by agitating it too much.

Felting (or "making felt") occurs when animal fibres are subjected to heat and friction, often using soap or detergent to help speed up the process. So if the aim is to *wash*, not to *felt*, water temperature and agitation must be kept to a minimum. It is best to use tepid water, and to lower small amounts of fleece carefully in to it, swishing it slowly through the soapy water. A netting bag, such as an onion bag, can be handy for this as it keeps the fleece together but lets the water wash through.

Once the fleece is washed it must be rinsed and then spread out to dry. Your skirting table can be useful for this as it lets air flow underneath, but make sure that any wire netting does not become rusty under the wet fleece. And remember that once the fleece starts to dry out it will become light and fluffy, and could blow away in even a gentle breeze.

Carding

The carding process takes the staples or locks of fleece and opens them up. You can card your own fleeces using a pair of hand carders or a drum carder, but this is quite a slow process and the end result is that you will have a lot of small *rolags* of carded fleece which will not be as even in size and easy to work with as professionally carded fleece. However, not only is it the cheaper option, but you may gain satisfaction from carrying out the whole process yourself.

Spinning

Once your fleece has been spun into yarn you can weave, knit or crochet it into scarves, garments or furnishings. You can either spin your fleece yourself or get someone else to do it for you. If you get someone else to do it, you might ask a home spinner, or you might take it to a mill to have it professionally spun.

The problem with commercial mills is that in most cases they require hundreds of kilos of any one batch of fleece before they will spin it. If you have just a few alpacas, and the fleeces are different colours and qualities, you cannot provide them with anywhere near a large enough quantity. There are some mills that specialise in single fleeces but of course the cost per kilo to spin these will be much higher than it would in a fully commercial mill. However the end result will be an evenly spun yarn from your own alpaca which you will be able to use. These mills usually offer a range of thicknesses for the finished yarn.

If you own a spinning wheel you can spin your own fleece - it is a very relaxing and satisfying thing to do. It is not difficult to learn to spin, but it can be a bit frustrating until you have the knack. Spinning is just a co-ordination of hands and feet, once you "have it", it is easy.

Spinning wheels were very popular during World War II as people spun wool and knitted for soldiers, but after the war the production of spinning wheels declined.

However, an interest in spinning revived in the late 1960's and 1970's, and wheels were then produced in some volume. If you do not own a spinning wheel it is easy to buy a second hand one that was made at that time. They are available for very reasonable prices and most are still in excellent working condition.

Learning to spin is easiest if someone shows you, rather than trying to learn from a book. There are spinning groups dotted all over the country, they meet regularly and usually welcome new members.

There is a myth amongst sheep's wool spinners that alpaca is difficult to spin. It is not. Suri is slippery and should be slightly overspun, but you will soon learn how best to spin your own fleeces to obtain the result you want.

Below: novelty yarn from white huacaya (spun thick) and black suri (spun fine) and plied to give a chunky bobble effect.

On the opposite page is Savannah, below is yarn hand spun from her fleece, and above a scarf knitted from that yarn. The fleece usually appears darker when spun than it does on the animal.

Felting

A fast and easy way to make useable fabric from your fleece is to felt it. You can felt coarser fleeces to make bags and hats and you can felt finer fleeces to make fine lightweight scarves. It is much easier to make felt from carded fleece than it is from raw fleece, but raw fleece can also be used.

Wet felting uses heat and friction to open the scales on the outside of the fibre, and when the scales close down again they lock the fibres together.

The technique of felting involves layering the carded fleece so that the first layer runs one way and the next layer runs the opposite way, and the third layer runs the same way as the first. The fleece must be placed carefully and evenly and then sprayed with hot soapy water and gently pushed down to form a wet mat of fleece. The easiest way to make felt is to use a large sheet of bubble wrap, and lay the fleece on half of it, folding the other half back on top of the fleece once it is wet and soapy. Once the fleece has made a wet mat you can start to work it more vigorously, kneading the bubble wrap into the fleece (but be careful not to

Opposite: a collection of felt pieces
Below: a wet felted scarf

disturb the layout of your fleece until it starts to hold together). The next step is to roll up the bubble wrap with the felt inside it, and then, putting as much pressure as you can on the roll, to knead it with your hands, rolling it backwards and forwards over and over again. The bubble wrap is then unrolled and rolled the other way, and the procedure is repeated. This continues until the felt is at the desired stage of firmness.

The more the felt is worked the stiffer it becomes. If you want a firm felt for a hat you will need to continue felting for much longer than if you want a soft draping scarf.

With wet felting the fleece becomes felt quite quickly. It is then washed and either laid flat to dry or moulded into the desired shape.

Another felting technique is *needle felting*. This uses a felting needle which has fine barbs along the sides, and the needle is repeatedly punched into the dry fleece and drawn back out again, causing the fibres to lock together.

Needle felting can be used to apply decoration to garments or furnishings, or to make three dimensional models.

Below: two handbags, made using the wet felting technique

When you are needle felting, place a thick piece of sponge or foam beneath your work, and stab the needle through the fleece into this.

The needle tip is very sharp so keep your fingers out of the way!

Right: two felting needles

Below: tip of felting needle, enlarged to show barbs, and models made using the needle felting technique

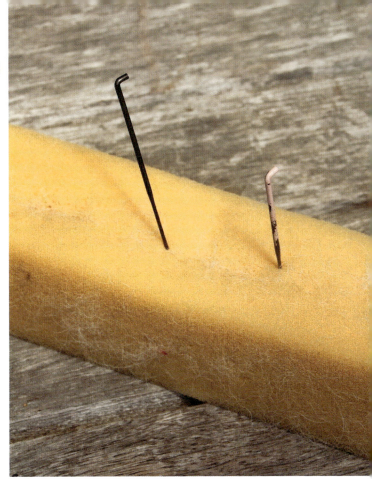

A
abnormal temperature 58
Accoyo 11
alarm call 22, 26
anaemia 46
annoying plants 40

B
background 9
barbed wire 30
barbers pole worm 46
behaviour 16
BEWs 85 - 87
birthing 67 - 72
black alpacas 83 - 88
blue eyed whites 85 - 87
body scoring 43
bottle feeding 76 - 77
breeding 64
breeding age 64
breeding anatomy 64
breeding for colour 83 - 91
broken bones 56
brown alpacas 84 - 88

C
cama 11
camelids 9
camels 9
carding 106, 108
cats 21
CF 63
coccidia 44, 46
colostrum 69
communications 25
cooling down 19
cria 75 - 80
cria coats 78 - 79
cria weight 75
CRV 63
CV 63

D
diary (of the herd) 23
dock 40
Dogs 21
Don Julio Barreda 11
dose rates 46
drenching 41, 44, 46
dung pile 20 - 21, 44 - 45
dust bath 19 - 20
dystocias 71, 72

E
E mac 46
ear positions 25
electric tape 32
endophyte 51
evolution 9

F
facial eczema 54 – 56
faecal egg counts 45
fancy alpacas 88
fat alpaca 43, 44
fawn alpacas 84 - 85
feeders 41
felting 110 - 113
Felting needle 112 - 113
fence height 30
fences 30 – 32
fighting 25
first imports 12
fleece contamination 40
fleece test results 62 - 63
fungal infections 53

G
gestation 64
grain overload 54
grey alpacas 83 -89

H
haemonchus 46
halter fit 26 - 27
halter training 26 - 29
handling 41
health 43– 58
herd behaviour 22
herd hierarchy 22
herd instinct 22
histograms 63
history 11
huacaya 10, 16
huacaya 14
humming 25

I
infections 58
injections 41, 61
ionophores 57 - 58

J
Johnes Disease 57

K
kush 16
Knock kneed cria 50

L
life cycle worms 44
life span 13
llama 8
loading into vehicle 26

M
magnesium deficiency 53
mating 64 - 67
mid side samples 61
mites 53
mouldy feed 57
moving 22, 26
moving fence 26

N
needle felting 112 - 113
newborn cria 69, 75, 76
nursing 75, 76

O
OFDA 2000 62
oleander 36
oral drenching 41
orgling 25, 66
ovulation 66

P
PEM 53, 54
pen mating 65
pen size 36,37
PF 63
phosphate deficiency 50
photographing 94- 97
placenta 69 - 71
poisoning 57 - 58
poisonous plants 36 - 37
posing for male 25
pregnancy 62 - 65
problem births 71 - 72
prolapse 72
puma 21

R
ragwort 37
rectal thermometer 58
rest homes 102
retained placenta 71

rhododendron 35
rickets 49 - 51
ruminants 12
ryegrass staggers 51 - 53

S
screeching 25
SD 63
SF 63
shade structures 34
shearing 60 - 61
shelter 33, 36
showing 92 - 93
sitting alone 58
skin conditions 53
skirting 104
skirting table 104 - 105
spinning 106 - 107
spit offs 67
spltting 16, 25
stocking ratio 30
suckling 75
sunbathing 18
sunburn 51
support groups 59
suri 10, 17
suri 15

T
tape worm 44 - 46
TB 57
teeth 49, 61
temperature range 56
thin alpaca 41, 42, 44
Tips (handling, feeders) 41
toenail trimming 47, 61
transporting 26

U
ultrasound scans 66
unpacking 67- 72
using the fleece 104 - 114
uterine horns 62

V
vicuna 10
visitors 20, 98 - 103
vitamin D3 49 - 51

W
washing fleece 105
weaning 80
wet felting 110 - 112

white alpacas 83 - 85
white marking genes 83 - 84
wild marking 90 - 91
worm life cycle 44
worming 44- 46

Y
yards and pens 32, 33

Notes and telephone numbers:

Made in the USA
San Bernardino, CA
12 December 2012